# A TIME
## OF OUR OWN
### In Celebration of Women Over Sixty

**Elinor Miller Greenberg and Fay Wadsworth Whitney**

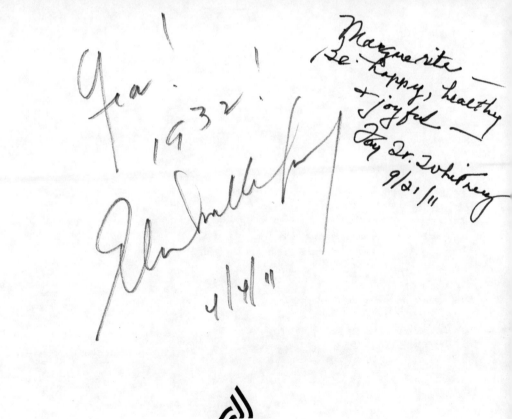

FULCRUM

GOLDEN, COLORADO

Library of Congress Cataloging-in-Publication Data

Greenberg, Elinor.
  Time of our own : in celebration of women over sixty / Elinor Miller Greenberg and Fay
Wadsworth Whitney.
     p. cm.
  Includes bibliographical references.
  ISBN 978-1-55591-644-2 (pbk.)
  1. Older women--United States.--Life skills guides.  I. Whitney, Fay W. II. Title.
  HQ1064.U5G692 2008
  646.7'90820973--dc22
                    2008013674

Printed in the United States of America by United Graphics Incorporated
0  9  8  7  6  5  4  3  2  1

Design by Jack Lenzo
Cover Image: © JupiterImages
"Life Is a Journey" by Rabbi Alvin I. Fine from *Gates of Repentance:
The New Union Prayerbook for the Days of Awe.* Copyright © 1978,
1996 by Central Conference of American Rabbis. Used by permission.

Fulcrum Publishing
4690 Table Mountain Drive, Suite 100
Golden, Colorado 80403
800-992-2908 • 303-277-1623
www.fulcrumbooks.com

This book could not have been written without the extensive educational and career experiences of both coauthors. And neither coauthor could have achieved her education and career goals without the support of four generations of family members:

Our parents, Sue and Ray Miller and Helen and Howard Wadsworth, who encouraged us to go to college and graduate school and to reach for careers that would be both interesting and satisfying for us individually, as well as beneficial to others in the world;

Our husbands, Manny Greenberg and Roy Whitney, who supported our returning to graduate school and going to work, even as we were raising our children and maintaining our households;

Our children, Andrea Greenberg, Julie Greenberg Richman, and Michael Greenberg; Lynne Allen, Paula Skrotzki, and Brian Whitney, who forgave us for missing some PTA meetings, car pools, and sporting events when we were working at night, leading meetings, and writing our doctoral dissertations.

And our grandchildren, Joshua and Adam Richman, Madeline and Alexandra Greenberg, Gerald Palmer, Whitney Palmer, Amanda Allen, Nick Skrotzki, Jeff Skrotzki, Erich Skrotzki, Anna Whitney, Aidan Whitney, Kyle Jordan, and Owen Whitney, who are growing up with the assumption that women can have both families and careers and still be the best grandmas, mothers, babysitters, and readers of bedtime stories in the world.

None of us does our work alone...

Nor without the support of loving and loyal families...

And, so, to our families, we say,

Thank you. We couldn't have done it without you. It is because of you, our families, that we are now enjoying full, healthy, and active lives, even as we move forward in the years beyond sixty...thriving in this new time of our own.

# Contents

The idea of this book began to germinate in 1992 when I, Ellie Greenberg, turned sixty. I had just completed writing *In Our Fifties: Voices of Men and Women Reinventing Their Lives* with two male colleagues. It seemed logical that the next edition, *In Our Sixties*, should follow. But that was not to be.

My sixtieth birthday proved to be so significant that I decided to celebrate it with a visit to a college roommate who lived in Mexico. The weeklong visit was spent doing some reminiscing, some touring, some talking, and a lot of writing. One excerpt from that writing follows.

> As I entered my sixties, I became aware of a deep, mysterious, and as yet undefined yearning for a little bit of wisdom—and enough time left in which to use it. The word *old* took on a new and more personal meaning, but I could not match my self-image—a perpetual twenty-two—with that meaning. I gave myself a sixtieth birthday present, a trip to Mexico, to visit my college roommate, my lifelong friend from our twenties, and perhaps to reclaim that youthful image of myself on which my mind had been fixed for almost forty years. Interestingly, I found that I could track the years in her life more accurately than in my own. We had giddy talks late into the night, sitting on the bed, just like we did at college. But our serious moments were now more about past losses than future gains—her loss of a husband and mother in recent years and my loss of a father and mother in past decades. Loss is a primary theme of our sixties, both the anticipatory fear of losing and the reality of it.
>
> Me—sixty! How could that be? Why, I'm just getting started. Hold it! Stop the clock! Where has the time gone? Is life really so very short?

One result of that sixtieth birthday retreat was the birth of the concept of "the third trimester of life," or "the third third of life," the period of time that begins at age sixty and extends for however long we might live. It was becoming clear that, at age sixty, a whole new set of issues begins to appear:

- How long will I be able to maintain my career?
- Will I experience age discrimination?
- Will I be able to continue to earn enough money?
- Who will hire me at this age?
- When will I retire? What will I do with my time when I retire?
- Will we have enough money when both my husband and I stop working?
- When shall I begin to collect Social Security?
- How does Medicare work, and when will I be eligible for it?
- How do my retirement benefits work?
- What will we be able to afford?
- Will my husband stay healthy? Will he continue to work or will he retire?
- What will he do when he retires?
- Will all my children marry? Will they stay married?
- Will I have grandchildren? How many? Boys or girls? Where will they live? How often will I see them?
- Will we stay in our current old family house or move into a smaller house or condo?

The questions seemed endless, and the answers were elusive.

It was becoming clear that this sixties decade was what Gail Sheehy in *Passages: Predictable Crises of Adult Life* refers to as a "deadline decade," a time for major decision-making, and that, in many ways, the sixties decade was going to be qualitatively different from the fifties decade that I had so recently lived through and studied for our book. Still, we did not have an adequate vocabulary to describe this period of time. In terms of adult development theory—the field of study and research that I had been working in for almost forty years—life after sixty for active women was clearly a new, relatively undescribed phase. Yes, there were books and studies in the field of geriatrics, but there was not much material or research on the "young old" or on the "new" generation of energetic and active women over sixty. Nor was there yet much writing on the kinds of mature lifestyles that were now being redefined and that could serve as role models for the 78 million baby boomers, the oldest of whom began to turn sixty in 2006.

It was becoming clear to me that the entire life cycle, as viewed from the other side of sixty, was beginning to look like three very different thirty-year periods: from birth to age thirty, from age thirty to sixty, and from age sixty to whenever one died. Even life beyond ninety was becoming relatively common.

For me, the questions and issues of women's lives after sixty were both personal and professional and could not be ignored. Since age thirty-nine, I had been a well-known and successful designer and administrator of innovative, high-quality higher education programs for adults that were based on my knowledge of adult development theory and practice. Most of my students were women. My doctorate and almost forty years of research were in the areas of adult development and adult learning. Yet little was known about adult or women's development after age sixty. The literature seemed to focus on two aspects of life: health and investments for retirement. Little was being written about the new breed of energetic and active women who were now turning sixty, those in the third third, or third trimester, of their lives.

Still, daily work and family priorities took precedence over starting a new research project and writing another book. So, for me, the study of issues of women over sixty was put on hold while I began to live out those years myself, writing a few articles, starting a new job, and beginning to listen carefully to other women over sixty, now in the third third of their lives.

During the same time frame, coauthor Fay Whitney was finding ways to combine her practice as a nurse practitioner, researcher, and teacher at the State University of New York Upstate Medical Center in

Syracuse, New York, following her reentry into the work world. Beginning in 1972 and during her thirties and forties, when she returned to work and school and was spending her first fifteen years as a nurse practitioner and educator, Fay had been involved in a new primary-care-provider movement in nursing. During that time, she had been creating and participating in many "firsts." They ranged from having her own first-career jitters while raising three teenagers to attending to a busy husband and completing her PhD. The career choice she made led her to creating and implementing new legislation and curricula for advanced nursing practice. She was involved in educating one of the first cadres of adult, pediatric, acute care, and geriatric nurse practitioners in the nation.

Fay was definitely "now" oriented, and in her forties and fifties, the most pressing questions for her revolved around how to build a career within the context of family obligations. Her descriptor for this period of life and developing career was "on the edge and in the front." Fay had reentered her nursing field twelve years after the career women of her time and felt pressured that she was behind. She persistently wondered, "What will be needed to catch up with my peers who have been working during all the years that I have not? Will I be able to do it?"

Entering her fifties, Fay had a new PhD behind her name and was just beginning a career-expansion phase of her work. It was a busy and exciting time. In the process of establishing herself as a nurse practitioner-educator-postdoctoral student, she arrived at the University of Pennsylvania School of Nursing to become one of nine members of the first class in the nation of Robert Wood Johnson Clinical Nurse Scholars. This required moving to a new state, establishing a research trajectory, developing a cadre of peers and colleagues, living in a city for the first time, and being in a challenging and often misunderstood faculty role. Looking back at that time, she says, "Developmentally, I was in the thirty- to forty-year-old career-building decade; in actuality, I was fifty. There was a two-decade disparity between my 'career' age and my actual age. I wondered how I was going to handle this."

Indeed, it was adapting to this new disparity that brought age-related questions to the fore. Never concerned about aging itself, Fay says she found herself researching strokes and working in a practice that involved elders and their families. Her patients were experiencing life-changing events that often occurred suddenly and could have irreversible effects. Aging and its consequences became a focus of Fay's learning and work, and it has continued to be to this day.

During that time, around her fifty-eighth birthday, Fay realized that she had become personally age conscious. Her mother had died at age fifty-eight, and she was determined not to die at that age too. So when she turned sixty, it was a positive milestone. At that same time, she had also made a huge change in her life by moving to Wyoming and becoming part of a rural campus at the University of Wyoming. It was there that we met.

Between 1992 and 1996, each of us was busy with our respective careers and families when our lives began to intertwine. Just when many people are planning to retire, at age sixty-four I began a new job as regional coordinator of the Mountain and Plains Partnership (MAPP). This partnership between sixteen institutions of higher-education and health-related agencies was created to design and deliver distance learning and online course–based master's degree programs to underserved rural and urban areas of Colorado, Wyoming, Arizona, and New Mexico, where adult students who wanted to become nurse practitioners, certified nurse-midwives, or physician assistants could be identified and enrolled in the higher education institution of their choice. Fay served the partnership as the representative from the School of Nursing at the University of Wyoming and covered the entire state of Wyoming for the project. I was based at the University of Colorado Health Sciences Center on the Anschutz Medical Campus in Aurora, Colorado.

As we began to work together, we recognized that we shared a developmental perspective on adult learning and the life cycle and that we were both experienced in qualitative research. As our colleagueship and friendship grew, we began to explore not only the developmental and professional challenges faced by our adult students, but also the issues now appearing in our own maturing life cycle development. After our work on the MAPP project was completed six years later, we each turned our attention to interests that had been put on hold, such as women's issues in the lengthening third third of life and the community-based health care needs of elderly women. And, as is often the case with women, our growing personal and professional relationship spawned another idea, in our case the concept of this book: to explore and celebrate the lives of contemporary women over sixty who are now, at the beginning of the twenty-first century, redefining and reinventing the third and final chapters of their lives.

In order to carry out our collaborative writing plan, we conducted forty one-to-one interviews with women between the ages of fifty-nine and ninety-two, born between 1914 and 1947. These interviews were focused on the topics addressed in this book. In addition, Fay held a series of small-group workshops on health issues. These studies were not scientifically designed with a stratified sample of the population, nor were they intended to represent statistically the entire universe of women in this age group. For the most part, the interviewees were middle-class American women who had lived very diverse lives that included both work and family as well as community activities.

Most of our interviews were conducted in person; a few with women at a distance were held over the telephone. Each interview took about two hours. The interview protocol matched the sequence of the chapters of this book, including questions and probes about (1) the concept of the third third of life, (2) redefining and reinventing life after sixty, (3) new roles, responsibilities, and relationships after sixty, including the roles of religion and spirituality, (4) issues of work and volunteerism, (5) money matters, (6) health issues, (7) losses, regrets, and gains at this stage of life, (8) new attitudes and advice to the baby boomers, and (9) a review and the future. The interview questions and probes can be found in Appendix A. A sample of the topics for the small groups is located in Appendix B, some reliable Web-based health resources are in Appendix C, and some seminar ideas and workshop exercises are in Appendix D. The interviewees were eager to share their ideas and insights and were very generous with their time and energy, two of our most precious and limited commodities.

The small groups were held weekly over a period of four years, between January 2002 and April 2007. They were held in Florida and included a majority of women and a few men. Attendance was at the discretion of the individuals, and so the number of attendees ranged from twelve to twenty-five at each meeting. The groups remained remarkably stable and interested over the five-year span, and they became a very interesting forum in which to discuss current health problems common among the participants as well as new advances in other areas of health care. The format included a brief prepared talk with handouts, when appropriate, followed by questions and input from the participants. The topics of interest ranged from the latest information about new or discontinued drugs to the problems of alcohol use among older people. The discussions were lively and very candid, producing rich information about what health concerns most of the participants had themselves, what problems they might be having with the health care system, and what friends and family members were doing to maintain healthy and functional lifestyles as they grew older.

It is significant that many of the women who were interviewed or participated in the small groups for this book not only lived their adult lives during the women's movement of the 1960s and 1970s but played leading roles in defining and advancing the goals of that movement. They were, in truth, the pacesetters in inventing new ways to balance family, work, and community activities during the increasingly complex second cycle of their adult lives, from about age thirty to age sixty. These are the women who created the new multi-role lifestyles that are now accepted as the norm. They have become role models not only for their own daughters, but also for baby-boomer women, born between 1946 and 1964, who are among that large culture-defining group of 78 million Americans just now beginning to turn sixty. Our interviewees and small-group participants are reusing the skills they acquired at a younger age and are playing leadership roles in redefining the third

third of women's lives, just as they redefined the second third when they were in their midlife years. These mature women over sixty are, once again, on the pioneering edge of change as they reinvent and redefine the years from age sixty to the end of life.

By combining and analyzing our interviews and small-group discussions with women from their late fifties to their early nineties, in addition to our day-to-day experiences with friends and colleagues and our own observations, we have sought to better understand and describe the issues and challenges of this evolving third third of women's lives. In doing so, we hope to have offered some fresh insights to those currently living through their mature years and to have shed some light on the future for the baby boomers.

In many ways, our lives are defined by the concept of time. At the start of a new year and at each birthday, we ask ourselves, "Where did the time go?" "Did I use my time well last year?" "What did I do that was good?" "What did I not do?" "What will I do next year?" As the years yet to live become fewer, we are especially mindful of the limits of the time we have left. The resource of time is finite, but its limits unknowable. We cannot make more of it. All we can do is manage it and make the best use of it that we can.

To manage time is to manage our identity. What we do becomes who we are. We may never quite grasp the elusive concept of time. But unless we are able to decide what is important to do with each moment each year, we may find ourselves bereft of the most precious and scarce resource any of us have. This is the one moment in history in which we live—our time.

And in this third and final period of our lives, we are, in fact, claiming a time of our own.

# Chapter 1

# The Third Third of Life

**When you get to my age, we've had more
yesterdays than we have tomorrows.**
—Former president William Jefferson Clinton,
age sixty, *Nightline*, July 31, 2007

As we enter our sixties, a new awareness comes over us: there are really three thirds, or phases, in our lives. Using time and age as our framework, we can discern that from birth to age thirty were our growing-up years, from thirty to sixty were our adult midlife years, and from sixty until we die are our older years. We may also realize that of the three phases, we know the least about the third third, a phase that older women today are exploring, redefining, and reinventing. We know the least about these older years because they are unprecedented. Never before have human beings lived so long in such good health and with such an abundance of resources at their disposal. And there has never been a time in which women, in every phase of their lives, have had the opportunities that today's women have.

As these conditions converge, there is a decided shift of consciousness as we enter our sixties. Health becomes a primary value and preoccupation. Money worries us more than ever. Our careers and work are destined to end shortly, and we wonder when we will be able to retire—or if we even want to retire. Our grown children are in their adult midlives, their second third of life, advancing in their careers and establishing families. We begin to focus on our grandchildren, if we are lucky enough to have some, who are in their growing-up years. Our relationship with our spouse or partner may change dramatically in either negative or positive ways, grow stronger, or end. If he or she is no longer in our lives, we create ties among others in an effort to replace the intimacy and stability our former relationship usually provided.

Our prominence in the community diminishes, and we pass the torch to younger leaders and try to become their mentors, not their competitors. Most of us have lost our parents and find ourselves to be the older generation. Fewer people actually remember the wars we have lived through: World War II, Korea, Vietnam. The more contemporary wars in Afghanistan and Iraq may trouble us differently than those of the past, yet to many they trigger memories of the same issues women have always had with war and its destruction. Still fewer have memories of being active in the civil rights movement, the peace movement, or the women's movement. We wonder if midcentury history—the Holocaust, the War on Poverty, the first atomic bomb—will be known at all by today's youth, if those events are being taught in schools, and, if not, what kind of society young people will create without these lessons.

## The Human Life Cycle

Throughout the centuries, philosophers, poets, playwrights, writers, and religionists have shed light on the various stages of life and the important matters that come before human beings as they live out their lives from birth to death. In addition, by the mid-twentieth century, an enormous body of research and literature about adult development became part of the field of developmental psychology and began to explain, in increasing detail, the various stages of what we now call "the human life cycle." However, the focus of developmentalists was on the first and second thirds of life. The third third, the years after age sixty, were considered to belong in the field of geriatrics, not adult development. This schism has created a false idea that after sixty, development ceases. In fact, those who work with our oldest populations know that this final third of life is highly creative and satisfying for many. Our own interviewees and groups further show that this is a lively developmental stage of life.

Recent literature, whether in the biologic, genetic, social, or psychological sciences, is beginning to reflect the many positive qualities of life over age sixty. We are all learning to change our stereotypes of older individuals and finding this new picture of life over sixty to be

2

much truer to reality as we ourselves move through our later decades. Perhaps *age* is coming of age!

In 1980, Rita Weathersby and Jill Tarule summarized and synthesized the major findings of many life cycle researchers of the 1950s through the 1970s in a publication of the Education Resources Information Center Clearinghouse on Higher Education and the American Association of Higher Education. Some of the researchers and writers of this period who established the vocabulary that we now use to discuss adult development and the life cycle were Arthur Chickering, Erik H. Erikson, Roger Gould, Robert Havighurst, Daniel Levinson, Bernice Neugarten, and Gail Sheehy.

A few key terms from that vocabulary are *life phase*, which is an age-linked period of time in which certain issues and tasks become primary; *marker events*, which are occurrences that set off, or trigger, particular issues and tasks; and *developmental tasks*, which occur in each life phase and can be undertaken unconsciously. Some developmental tasks are actually linked to external marker events, while others are psychological, individual, and internal in nature.

## The First Third of Life

Erikson focused his attention on our first thirty years, from birth to early adulthood. We understand that first third as primarily revolving around physical growth and maturation, as we progress from infancy to childhood, through adolescence, and forward to early adulthood. Accompanying this life phase of increasing physical size and strength are various psychological issues, or developmental tasks, that Erikson portrayed as the development of trust, autonomy, initiative, industry, identity, role clarification, and, finally, intimacy, as opposed to isolation. We can see from Erikson's perspective that in our first third we are engaged in the development of our own individual selves while, at the same time, we are learning to develop and carry out our developing relationships with others.

In synthesizing various life cycle models, Weathersby and Tarule gave us descriptors for many of the later substages of the first third of life. They charted the characteristics of the "leaving the family" stage, usually between the ages of sixteen and twenty-four, when going to college or work often generates new living arrangements. Being in a peer group is important as one's adult identity is being shaped in our early adulthood. Then comes the "getting into the adult world" stage, at about age twenty to twenty-nine. During this time, we make tentative commitments to a career, often start our first job, seek a mate, and begin to have children and build a family. The age-thirty transition, which can last anywhere from a few months to a decade, often requires a reexamination of the questions "What's life all about?" and "What do I want out of life?" Strains on marriage in this transitional period may lead to divorce or separation. The challenges of adult transitions become apparent in our early thirties and will become even more apparent in future years as transitions occur cyclically throughout our adult lives.

## The Second Third of Life

Erikson views the major developmental task of the second third of life, our adult midlife years, as being "generativity" versus stagnation. This means that during the years from ages thirty to sixty, we are constantly seeking ways to energize and reenergize our lives. We often marry, have children, find work, and become active members of our communities. These are usually our most productive years, our "make it or break it" years. In these thirty years we take all the growth, maturity, education, skills, financial resources, and relationships that we have been able to muster thus far and employ them to establish our lifestyles, create our families, and build our careers. We view the most successful among us as those who have been able to negotiate this period of time with the greatest amount of satisfaction and the least amount of failure. If we have been able to be generative, according to Erikson's terms, we are continually able to renew ourselves and those around us. If we are generative, we have gained the capacity for creativity, reinvention, and rejuvenation. The alternative is stagnation, lack of progress and a humdrum, unsatisfactory adult life.

In Weathersby and Tarule's scheme, early adulthood, or the second third of life, is characterized by a series of maturations. In our early thirties, we settle down and make deeper commitments to work and family. We create stability, are concerned with "making it," and begin to meet our long-term goals. Between about ages thirty-five and forty-two, we are becoming our own person as we establish and maintain work and family roles. We may reach out to play broader community roles during this period: run for political office, volunteer regularly, or become involved in church or synagogue life. Midlife transitions characterize the early forties as the connection between early choices and current reality begins to weaken. Restlessness and change often disrupt marriage, family, and work. Divorce becomes more common. Restabilization begins to occur around age forty-five, when new interests, relationships, and friendships add to the enjoyment of life once again.

The transition into the decade of our fifties contains another jolt of reexamination and redirection as we realize that we have already lived through our own personal half century and, from this point on, the time to yet live is less than the time already lived. The fifties have been seen as a "last chance" decade, partially because they have been labeled thus in the literature. Perhaps as we get more informed about this extended phase of life where living into one's seventies and eighties is commonplace, we will all redefine again what the "last chance" stage of life is. But we do know that the fifties are a difficult decade for many. During this time, some flee their marriages for new relationships; others make significant work changes. There's a "hurry up" sense, and we get very busy being very busy. In the late fifties, there is often a restabilization and mellowing as we begin to get more comfortable with our older selves, our spouses, and our own adult midlife-aged children. We begin to set new goals for the time left to live. Sometimes these goals are implicit and not articulated; other times we state our new goals and act on them. We say things like, "Before I go, I must finish my college degree," and then we return to school to complete that goal. Or we might say, "When I was young, I was a pretty good artist. I miss my art," and then we begin a new sculpture class and show our art in local galleries. There is a new sense of urgency to do those things that have been put off for years. Our fifties are a new kind of "me" decade, with the feeling that now that the children are grown and on their own, it's our turn.

## The Third Third of Life

Here's where the developmental literature gets a bit thin. It is often said that adult development researchers like to study the years up to their own ages, but rarely go beyond those years. Weathersby and Tarule lump the sixties and the years beyond as a period of "life review and finishing up." The major psychic tasks of this period, they say, are "accepting what has transpired in life as having worth and meaning; valuing oneself and one's choices." The marker events of the years after sixty are retirement, for both women and their spouses, aging, and death, of friends, spouses, and, finally, oneself. And the characteristic stance of the years after sixty is a "review of accomplishments [and] eagerness to share everyday human joys and sorrows; family is important; death is a new presence."[1]

Although these descriptors seem rather brief to cover a period of time of thirty years or more, other writers say even less. Chickering and Havighurst base their work on that of Neugarten and show a blank on their chart of typical life changes for women over sixty. When describing men over sixty, these researchers generally say that men become more nurturing and pay more attention to relationships as they grow older. Of the years between fifty-five and seventy-five, they say, "[The] time left to live is limited, and life tasks must be completed. Death [is] expected [but there is] nothing to dread provided it comes 'on time.'"[2] Levinson barely goes beyond his own mid-forties age in *The Seasons of a Man's Life*; his section of the chart is blank from age forty-five onward. The same is true of Sheehy in the very popular 1976 book *Passages: Predictable Crises of Adult Life*; the chart is blank after age fifty. Her final chapter, titled "Renewal," is about the middle years and does not discuss the older years after age sixty. Her 1995 sequel, *New Passages: Mapping Life across Time*, has a final chapter titled "Passage to the Age of Integrity," which talks about the "Serene Sixties," the "Sage Seventies," the "Uninhibited Eighties," the "Nobility of the Nineties," and the "Celebratory Centenarians." That's getting close, but it still does not get at the core issues of women's lives during the third third of life today, a mere dozen years after Sheehy wrote *New Passages*.

## Experiencing the Third Third of Life: Our Interviewees

When we began the interviews for this book, we were not certain if the concept of the third third of life would be meaningful and accurate for our interviewees. So we asked them at the outset, "When you hear me describe this time of your life as the third third of life, what does it make you think of?" For the most part, the interviewees liked the concept very much. They called this way of looking at their years after age sixty wonderful, sensible, busy, exciting, and challenging and said that this cycle of life implied freedom. Some said that they expected to live to be ninety or one hundred years old.

One interviewee, a seventy-seven-year-old native of Chile, spoke of the cultural differences between her country and the United States: "Women in Chile at this age are just sitting around," she said, "and like a painting on the wall, they are looking down on what's going on. I am doing a tremendous amount of work, more than when I worked for pay. I am like a jumping fish. I don't have enough time to do it all."

We asked, "How would you broadly characterize the time of your life after sixty and how would you label it?" Their answers were remarkably upbeat. They loved their sixties and had found new freedom after their children had grown up and were on their own. Many found their sixties to be the peak of their professional careers. They also had the opportunity to travel, often worldwide, were seen as experts in their fields, could work alone at home in a quiet environment, had energy and enthusiasm for what they were doing, and were glad to be getting off the organizational racetrack of their earlier years. They were working at their own pace on the things they cared about and were open to the flow of new opportunities, unfettered by rules and "shoulds." Most were comfortable with themselves and more at ease than in previous periods of their lives.

Our interviewees focused first on the positive sides of life after sixty. However, despite their pleasure with life after sixty, almost all of them had experienced, or were currently facing, serious health challenges. A number of them had fought various types of cancer and survived thus far. One interviewee was receiving treatment for Parkinson's disease, which had severely limited her physical strength and coordination. Others had endured brain tumors, vertigo, back problems, and neurological diseases. Still, they continued to teach, write, do research, give speeches, lead workshops, design and produce jewelry, provide beauty care, travel, and care for themselves and their families. In spite of their physical challenges, as a group they had continued to adopt optimistic attitudes, stay busy with activities they enjoyed, and, overall, were models of a new breed of third-third women.

We probed further and asked, "Are there specific characteristics of this age that you think most women could agree on? What are they?" They replied, "This is our time" without being prompted. "My kids have gone and now I'm free to be creative and active," said one interviewee. "I am respected, have seniority, and am honored," said another. "I'm more introspective and 'doing my own thing,'" reported a woman who had been a public figure.

Although some were unable to do physically what they used to do, others were playing tennis, skiing, swimming, running, doing yoga, and hiking. Almost all had an exercise program. They were consciously taking care of themselves and interested in living as long and as well as possible.

Some of the interviewees had experienced the death of a spouse, a few had remarried, and others had adjusted to living alone. Some were caring for spouses whose health had deteriorated, and they were kept busy with medical appointments and care-giving activities. Still, they were grateful for having long-term relationships and remained loyal to their partners.

Overall, the third third of life for these women was an active and busy time. They had transcended the illnesses and deaths of spouses and conquered their own physical challenges. They were generally satisfied with their lives, were taking up new work and activities, and felt more at home with themselves than in prior stages of their lives. Most of them were experiencing a period of freedom, satisfaction, and creativity. They were not preoccupied with the end of their lives, but were taking hold of the time they had now and were using it well.

## Today's Women and the Life Cycle

Just as the women who we interviewed had led the way through the women's movement of the 1960s and 1970s during the first and second thirds of their lives, they were now plowing new ground in their third thirds.

They were not wallowing in life-review activities and memories. They were instead maximizing their health and embarking on new and exciting activities and doing so with a calm sense of confidence born of having succeeded in their prior years. They were excited about their newfound freedom and prepared to cope with whatever life had in store for them.

In short, the third third of their lives had truly become a time of their own.

# CHAPTER 2

# The Concept of Reinvention

**Art imitates nature, and necessity**
**is the mother of invention.**
—Richard Frank, *Northern Memoirs*,
written 1658, published 1694

## The *R* Words

Many women entering their sixth decade consider reaching retirement age as "facing the *R* word." To some, it means giving up a part of their life that they are glad to leave behind; to others, it presents a challenge that they look forward to as a new adventure. *Retirement* is a word that conjures up change, the uncertainty of the unknown, and a potential new phase of growth. Like other *R* words—regain, retread, renew, revisit, reestablish, relearn, remake, reintegrate—it may say, "Do it again...but this time, get it right!"

This time of life can best be described as a time of reinvention or redefinition of one's daily life and aspirations for the future. So we asked our interviewees what they thought about the concept of reinvention. It was exciting to hear their articulate and enthusiastic responses. In spite of the challenges they faced, they were remarkably upbeat. They understood that they were the first generation to be living such long and healthy lives. They met the challenges of health they faced with an expectation of recovering from their illnesses or living with their chronic conditions. They were actively planning and redefining various aspects of their lives to take advantage of the retirement years ahead of them. When we asked them to elaborate, they said that the third third of life was a time of:

- A different type of productivity
- Creativity

11

- A different growth pattern
- Another decade-change, each one being a time of reinvention
- Expecting to be healthy and working at it
- "Cashing in" on one's investments in life
- Blossoming of partner and family relationships
- Giving back to society
- Slowing down and appreciating the small things
- A resurgence of creative talents and a time "to be who I really am"
- Fewer role models
- A way to regain lost time from the past

But the term *reinvention* conjures up many ideas and does not fit everyone in quite the same way. Most of our interviewees saw their older decades as a definite transition time. For those retiring and leaving their employment status, this transition required much thought and planning. But many had made efforts to continue to work. For example, one interviewee, at age seventy-five, said, "I have reinvented myself altogether. Now, with my family grown and gone, all that I do is my teaching. I seem to think I'm in my forties when it comes to work. I get up at 4 AM to be at school at 6 AM, and I work at home grading papers at night. I'm not even associating with women my own age; my coteachers are in their thirties and forties."

Another interviewee, an eighty-eight-year-old woman who had created her own real estate business at a young age, after her husband passed away, made a business transition during her seventies and eighties. She had been able to let go of the real estate business when it became physically too taxing, and then she created a new hat business. "Fashion as a passion," she joked. She was using some of the dependable people she had trained and employed in real estate to do the "detail work" in her hat business. Wearing an outrageous hat to our interview, she mentioned that her love of fashion had never died when she was selling real estate, but what she was doing now was much more "her." She was now dealing with people who respected her fanciful side, which she believed had made her successful in selling houses with a flair. No doubt she was right on target with that assessment. And she was delightful.

While a surprising number of our interviewees were crafting new ways to continue to work or starting new ventures based on their lifetimes of experience, there were also many who were glad to be free from working. It seems that we each dream of a time when we will, once again, have the freedom of childhood, when responsibilities were not our primary concern and playful and imaginative ideas could grow into wonderful games and memories. Yet we are different after sixty, and many resources and experiences factor into our ability to react to the possibility of a major change in our daily routine and future development. Whatever reaction we may have initially, the prospect of reinvention is a daring and wonderfully freeing concept that needs to be looked at and turned over in our minds until it fits our present ambitions and state of affairs.

One interviewee was eloquent about her ideas of this transitional time. She saw each decade as having the opportunity to add depth to the person she had become, to give her the time to think, to concentrate, and to make each time of change pivotal. She said that "few people ever really make the very deep changes that come to mind when thinking about reinventing themselves, but most thoughtful people look at transitional changes as a time to gain new self-knowledge and adapt their actions and dreams to new circumstances." As a theater artist in her younger years, she had learned how to "invade the psyche of the characters" she had played and found this a useful life skill later, when she pursued a social work career in midlife. Now in the process of obtaining a PhD in adult education, she found herself using those same theater skills in listening to and entering into the lives of her students in order to best teach them at their individual learning levels. She felt that her skills were gaining depth with each life transition, and she was glad to have this opportune time in life to change course and do things in a different way, in a different place, and with different stakes and outcomes. She said that she loved this time of life and that she was a "joyous example" of how women make changes in a "fabulous way," with enthusiasm and energy.

## Our Mothers, Ourselves

After clarifying the definition of reinvention, we asked each interviewee, "Thinking about yourself and your peers in relation to women in your mother's generation, what might be some similarities and differences between the two generations?"

"We are much younger and more vibrant and daring than our parents," said one interviewee in her eighties. Another woman, in her mid-seventies, stated, "I'm much younger than my mother was at this age. I enjoy doing physical work like regrouting, tiling, and repairing the carpet; I'm physically in good condition."

As we probed further, we began to confirm our hunches about the concept of reinvention or redefinition of current women's lives in the third-third years. Not surprisingly, most of our interviewees described their mothers' lives as those of traditional homemakers. Most of their mothers had not worked outside the home, had limited education, and found their identities through their husbands. This was typical of women's circumstances in the early and mid-twentieth century in America. Compared to the women of the previous generation, today's women over sixty had experienced many more options in their lives: more education, more financial resources, more career opportunities, and more varied lifestyles and marital choices.

Not only were their mothers more traditional, but our interviewees' entire early family life reflected traditional habits: the extended family ate dinner together every Sunday, mother got dressed properly every morning, even if she was staying home, and dinner was on the table every night at the agreed-upon time, when the father came home from work. For most of the women in our study, life in their childhood looked like a Norman Rockwell painting.

However, there were exceptions. Some of our interviewees had nontraditional mothers who were divorced, worked, were active in politics, or behaved like Auntie Mame. When one interviewee spoke about her mother, she said, "My mother was Auntie Mame! She was years ahead of her contemporaries. When she was widowed at age fifty-one, she went on a cruise around the world and took stunning photos. She'd say to me, 'If you don't do it, shame on you!'" That mother was a role model for her now spirited and independent seventy-six-year-old twice-widowed daughter. On the other hand, a few of our interviewees had lost their mothers when they were very young. Those women expressed sadness and were sorry that they had not been able to share their lives with their mothers. One interviewee recalled, "My mother died at the age of forty-eight from breast cancer. I was in the second grade. Then my father died too, and I was brought up by my aunts. I was an only child and did not have any real parents. I was very lonely." Today that woman is in her early sixties and is very skilled at reinventing her life at every stage. The difficult circumstances of her early years caused her to develop into a very independent and self-sufficient adult. As a result, she has continued the process of redefinition throughout her life. Turning sixty was just another transition in a long line of transitions.

All of the women with whom we talked agreed that they had many advantages compared to their mothers: they were living longer, they were more physically active, they had more education, they had more long-term career options and successes, and they were younger in their attitudes and healthier in the third third of their lives. As a result, they felt challenged to redefine their lives at this stage. And that is exactly what they were doing.

## The Definition of Reinvention
## in the Eyes of Our Interviewees

*Reinvention* was not a familiar word to our eldest interviewees. "I never thought of that word," said one ninety-one-year-old woman. She had left her farm home in Wyoming and was later considered to be a matriarch in the western states. Giving of her time and money to make life better for rural and international people through the development of

15

library resources, she elevated scores of lives beyond their original level. She created learning programs in very remote places and mentored young librarians in several library courses. She neither thought she had invented or reinvented anything of any note. She felt she had simply used her talents and resources to do what was right. She had managed to get a college education when few women did. She married twice, once to a minister who took her to Appalachia. There, she established libraries where there were none. Her second husband was a senator in her home state. Together they built financial success that allowed her to grow in her field of library science and become a philanthropist. Her philanthropy included the development of nine libraries in the Philippines. She became an internationally recognized scholar in her field. Having returned to her home state, she has continued her community service, which encompasses work with individual students as well as work on community health projects with a regional hospital. She still sees these activities as part of her life's work. As her health declines, she only regrets that she runs out of energy sooner than she used to, though her mind is still busy. Although she may not use the word *reinvention*, she has, indeed, redefined the third third of her life.

## The Anxiety of Redefinition

Another woman, in her early sixties, expressed a high level of anxiety as she anticipated retiring from her highly visible position: "I've been so defined by my job and community boards that I will have to totally redefine myself. I'm afraid that I won't be anybody! I'm concerned about how I will fill my days…and how I will get the intellectual stimulation I need."

The fear of loss of identity is commonly expressed by women who have been successful in their careers and who worry that they will become invisible when they give up their title and their office. In many ways, they are correct. And the more powerful they are, the more difficult it is to give up that power. At the same time, they yearn for more freedom and time to do things other than work. Having two pulls, both of them attractive, is called an "approach-approach conflict" by psychologists. These conflicts are no less stressful than choices between things we wish to avoid.

Another of our youngest interviewees, who had just turned sixty and whose work was less public but the center of her life nonetheless, said, "But what will I do every day if I am not working?" She simply could not envision getting up each morning and not going to work. She had no hobbies and little family. This person might profit from being involved in a small preretirement group where she could hear how other women were planning to make the transition to a nonworking life.

Entire preretirement workshops and courses are being held on these common concerns, often resulting in effective support groups as women move through the post-employment transition together. A retiree in her seventies who might also benefit from such support groups put it this way: "There are not many good models for women in their later years. People are lucky if they can continue what they want to do. Society hasn't figured it out. There's a mismatch between the time available and the possibilities for contributing to society." A case in point are many volunteer opportunities. Their old ways of thinking about volunteering often do not fit for experienced career women, even if they are interested in giving back to the community in some way. There is very limited personnel at most nonprofit agencies to counsel retirees and match them with meaningful volunteer activities. So many women, as well as men, face their retirement years without a plan for daily activities that interest them. This is an unmet need: helping those in their third third of life find ways to use their expertise and experience to help others while gaining meaning in their own lives.

## The Joy of Redefinition

Although some of our interviewees who were just approaching retirement expressed anxiety about their impending transition, others were truly joyful about this third third of life. They spoke of exciting scenarios about their reinventions and redefinitions with comments such as:

- "This is a time to reflect, to learn, and to give back."
- "It's my time, and I am going to make it great."
- "I'm not in a hurry like I was before."
- "This period of life is the time to do what I was meant to do."
- "[This is] the best time of my life. Just plain fun."

It is interesting that these women were enthusiastic about changes that were likely to occur when they retired. With fewer daily family, career, and social responsibilities, they planned to bring into being many interests from earlier in their lives that they would now be able to resurrect. They were positive and excited about these changes and the opportunities these years presented. Although some of our interviewees had not adopted our term *reinvention* regarding what they were doing, they were, in fact, reinventing themselves.

The women we interviewed thought today's women over sixty were new models of activity and health. Now that they had reached this age, they didn't view themselves the same way that they viewed their female predecessors. The terms they used to describe today's women over sixty were *vibrant, creative, contributors, innovators*, and *super citizens*. They saw themselves continuing to make change a part of their everyday life, rather than waiting for a special time to live differently.

## The Habits of Reinvention
## Born during the Women's Movement

Change had been part of these women's lives when they were younger, especially for those who saw themselves as an important part of the women's movement. Activity in the movement changed not only their own lives, but also altered their families' ideas of equality between genders. Husbands, sons, and daughters reconsidered the way they saw women and their roles. As a result, younger generations have a much broader view of women's contributions to society and their place in the world.

Even as these women cautioned that there was still much work to do to achieve full equality between the sexes, they hoped that younger women would take up the challenge. This third third of life and the prospect of having time in their retirement years to become role models for younger women was intriguing to some of our interviewees. One interviewee was very clear and said, "I want to be a role model for other women." It was especially energizing for some of them to think that reinvention could happen at any time in life and that in their later years, they might continue to influence younger women.

## Fear of the Unknown

One of the reasons many people shy away from ideas surrounding aging and retirement may be our fear of the unknown. This fear often prevents us from doing risky things. It is hard to put energy into redefining our daily lives when we are fearful of stepping into unfamiliar territory. But now that the number of older people is increasing as life expectancy rises and the 78 million baby boomers begin to move into their sixties, a critical mass is forming. Each day there are new ads, articles, and films about older people. More retirement homes are being built. The third third is becoming more familiar. As average life expectancies (ALE) have increased—now at 75.2 years for males and 80.4 years for females—our larger older population can provide us with much more experiential wisdom about what is to come.[1] The addition of 78 million baby boomers will change our demographics yet again. So it is not surprising that we worry about planning for the years our predecessors never reached. In order to reduce our fears, we must trust in our ability to adapt to changing circumstances. As the numbers increase, the issues and challenges of the third third of life will become more familiar and thus less fearsome. Somewhere in the not-too-distant future, a tipping point will be reached and many issues of the third third of life that now cause fear and anxiety will have become familiar and will no longer cause these levels of stress.

## Positive Aging

While for some the challenges of aging and retirement may be over-whelming, for others the third third is a freeing and positive time. Many of our interviewees mentioned the thrill of now having the time and inclination to be more daring in their thinking: "It's my time now, and I can do as I wish," one woman boasted. Instead of fear, she exhib-ited "positive aging."

Robert D. Hill describes the differences between normal aging, successful aging, and positive aging in an insightful and research-enriched book, *Positive Aging: A Guide for Mental Health Professionals and Consumers*. The book is precisely that—positive. Hill suggests that there are positive characteristics in people that make this reinvention experience both possible and rewarding. (For more information on positive aging, see Chapter 6, "Women and Health.") He stresses that putting these characteristics to work requires personal effort, a consis-tent, positive attitude, and continued development. As a result of our study, we suggest that the reasons some women have aged well may be these very characteristics that Hill identifies.

## New Models for Today

Today's aging women will most certainly leave behind footprints for other women to follow. Role models are now in the making for the next group of women, the baby boomers, who are just beginning to enter the third third of their lives. So we asked our interviewees, "What do women over sixty today believe are the new models for this stage of life?"

The answers came in a flood. First, they gave the physical descrip-tors of the "new" woman over sixty: strong, healthy, and doing regular exercises. Next came the behavioral characteristics: vibrant, daring, risk-taking, creative, self-confident, self-sufficient, and productive. In terms of what were some of the appropriate roles and activities dur-ing the third third of life, our interviewees answered, "to contribute, give back to the community, mentor, travel, find meaningful activity, associate with younger women, and invest in friendships." Continu-ing to work for as long as possible, perhaps on new schedules, was very important to some, while others preferred to reap the benefits of their careers and successes, accept their awards, and slow down. Most importantly, there was a virtual chorus of voices with inspiring statements such as:

- "This is my time."
- "Everything is new again; I'm loving it!"
- "This is my last chance to do what I want to do."
- "I'm finally settling in to who I am."
- "I'm not retiring just to play golf."
- "I don't care what others think; I'm going to be me."
- "We're all breaking new ground; we have a new voice, a collective voice with more power, a new reality, a new definition."
- "I'm now doing what I was meant to do."
- "I'm not in a hurry anymore."

One interviewee in her seventies put it this way: "Being a feminist, I believe women must realize that they are an important part of the population. They must develop their talents and contribute to the world…For so many years, women were second-class citizens… Women in this age group—and women of all ages—must realize what they have to offer."

Another interviewee, who was anticipating her retirement from a highly visible long-term responsible position, said, "I want an easier way of life. I want to reconnect with old friends, do new things, paint, do pottery, travel to [explore] other cultures, do gourmet cooking and entertain, raise flowers, and dance the tango." Another woman, who was recently divorced, took back her given name as a public statement of her new life. Yet another, who had recently remarried, was now "living life on her own terms" and described herself as "more self-confident." One woman said that she was learning how to be a widow, while a contemporary who was recently widowed was spending more time with her music and her piano students. Different life-changing marker events were providing these women with entirely new environments for new transitions, decisions, and redefinitions of every aspect of their lives. They were in the very profound process of reinventing themselves and their entire lives.

This is not trivial stuff. These times require courage and imagination, as well as perseverance and intelligence. None of us should underestimate the challenges that this third third of life represents.

These overwhelming attitudes of freedom and choice dominated the discussions with our interviewees. Many of these women cited the women's movement as having given them permission to live their lives on their own terms, and they were continuing in this mode in their older years, only in a more relaxed and confident way, without guilt, anxiety, or pressure to perform. They were more at peace and, at the same time, were excited about the many changes they were now able to make in their lives.

## The Inspiration of *Earth's Elders*

In a totally delightful book, *Earth's Elders: The Wisdom of the World's Oldest People*, Jerry Friedman expresses his wonder and delight about the worldwide phenomenon he "discovered" among the world's oldest people. A photographer by profession, he wandered the world for three years talking with the oldest living people, those over age one hundred, taking pictures of them, and being entranced by their stories. He wrote, "By Darwinian standards they had developed the crucial survival skill, the instinctual ability to reinvent themselves or to modify their lives" in order to maintain positive and productive attitudes and behaviors.[2] Perhaps the capacity for self-reinvention is one of those necessary characteristics of positive aging and another way of describing what Erik H. Erikson called "generativity."

Friedman was not a sociologist, gerontologist, or well-known literary giant. He was a photographer who immersed himself in a special population and learned from his subjects. He formulated a list of characteristics that he found in people with longevity all over the world:

- Optimism
- Genetic longevity
- Coping and adapting
- Prominence of family and family values
- Hard work
- Eating simply
- Faith, not just religiosity
- Living with and in nature
- Humor

Rather than revealing a fountain of youth or a plan one could follow to live a long life, Friedman saw life as "a puzzle, a mosaic of traits that forms a living code rather than a map."[3] This concept is intriguing. Our interviews reveal nearly the same things as did Friedman's, and our conclusions are very similar. Living long is complicated by the interferences of life, which change things. With the ability of humans to adapt, there are traits, circumstances, and events within individuals that allow their genetic makeup to keep them growing into very old age. It seems that this third third of life is just one piece of a larger puzzle, a puzzle in which each individual must find the pieces to make her life whole and rewarding. Life cannot be described or lived in a single dimension and must fit into a total puzzle, a puzzle we each uniquely construct. This is an uplifting thought and a challenge for us all.

Friedman's book includes wonderfully expressive faces and tales of living that astounded him for their variety and experiences. For him, even the sad revelation that some he had worked to find and tried to interview had died before he was able to reach them reinforced the notion that death is a part of living, with its own timetable. There was little regret among his subjects, regardless of their hurdles or accomplishments in life. Friedman's pictures are a study in smiles and wrinkles entwined, sparkling eyes in skins of different hues, and a peace that emanates from an understanding and faith in human strengths.

## Reinvention, Renewal, and Revival

All our interviewees had found this third third a time of major transition. Since they ranged in age from just turning sixty to over ninety, they were in different places in the cycle of transition.

As we continued our interview discussions and focused on the concept of reinvention, we asked about whether or not our interviewees were experiencing deepening ties with friends, partners, and others at this time of life. Some reported that they were taking time to reestablish ties with childhood friends; others were taking new acquaintances to lunch in order to nurture new friendships. Whether rediscovering old friends or expanding their horizons with new ones, spending time with friends had become more important and feasible, as their obligated hours decreased and their available hours increased. Husbands and wives were also spending more time together, and, in some cases, strengthening their relationships in new and enriching ways.

We also inquired about our interviewees' experiences with the revival of earlier or latent talents. Some of the women in their early sixties had had opportunities to renew old interests and talents: returning to act in the theater, painting, experimenting once again with other visual arts, and starting their own new businesses. Others were continuing what they had been doing for years, but in different ways: playing tennis and skiing, traveling, writing books, serving on boards, and continuing their work, but at a slower pace. One preretirement interviewee was anticipating her postretirement years and said dreamily, "I want to focus on my own talents, my own creativity. For me it's art, writing, and public speaking. Something is going to blossom. It feels good." Another said, "I'm just now defining my art. It's absolutely reinvention time."

## Grandparenting as Renewal

Our interviewees' role as grandma loomed high on their priority lists. As the grandchildren grew older, each grandmother found ways to continue to build strong relationships with them: traveling together, going to concerts and theater together, and even skiing together.

One woman moved everything in her life to be closer to her grandchildren: she changed countries, cities, jobs, careers, and associates. Most women agree that there is nothing like the experience of having grandchildren. These women relish the opportunities to care for and visit with their grandchildren and then go home and leave the children to their own parents. Those who had grandchildren living in the same town saw them very often, and those whose grandchildren were far away traveled as often as possible to see them. By the same token, those without grandchildren expressed a sense of loss and regret and frequently "adopted" others' grandchildren so they could share precious childhood years once again.

One example of this is the Foster Grandparent Program. This mutually federal- and state-funded program was developed to provide some income to women above sixty-five who fall into certain income brackets that may not be meeting their financial needs. The program is used in the K–12 educational system to tutor and support children who need the added attention to succeed. One of our interviewees who worked in the Foster Grandparents Program saw it as a "place to have grandkids I will never have" and definitely felt it was a way to give back to the next generation. Perhaps leaving something of value to younger generations is instinctive to people over sixty, especially women. The children who benefit need the attention and love they lack from an adult, and they easily share their love for their adopted grandparent. It is a win-win-win situation for the children, the foster grandparent, and society as a whole.

## Reinvention as a Result of Health Problems

When health problems interfered with our interviewees' plans, those women with serious chronic or acute illnesses had to reinvent their lives in less ambitious ways, with less physical activity, work, travel, and community participation. But like their contemporaries who were healthy and busy taking classes and lessons, participating in politics, and meeting friends for lunch, they were interested in their own next steps toward becoming more of "who they really are." For one interviewee in her early seventies whose husband had had a stroke and was increasingly dependent on her, daily concerns were quite pragmatic: "I need to be more self-sufficient regarding money, and I can't rely on my husband anymore. I have to make my own way. I view myself and my work differently. I plan to work for as long as my employer will let me."

Another had become a caretaker to her husband when what she had planned to be in retirement was an artist, a role she had filled earlier in life. Not educated as a nurse, she relied on her own ability to metamorphose into a new role, and she discovered she was good at it. She cared for her husband in his illness, and when he died, she went back to school at seventy years of age and became a nurse in gerontology.

When women themselves become ill or dependent, they suffer a huge reorganization of their lives. Generally the caregiver in the family, becoming more dependent on others is a great transition. One woman said, "I am struggling so hard not to become the 'old crabby lady,' but I am so mad that I am dependent on others when I was the one everyone depended upon. So they call me stubborn. Thank heavens for that or they would have all the care of me."

So reinvention for new roles is not always welcome. But women are very capable of making adjustments to new circumstances. Most of our interviewees were very good at this transition, even in their angst, and kept finding positive ways to cope.

## Women Helping Women Reinvent

It is true that necessity is the mother of invention. When we talk about reinventing our lives in the years after sixty, we are responding to the many necessities and new realities of women's lives. Those new realities are:

- Longer and healthier lives
- More and better education
- Varied and successful careers
- Experience with politics and government
- Service on volunteer boards and in the community

- Changed marital and family roles
- Heightened self-confidence and independence

Throughout the years, women have turned to other women for the guidance and support they might need, and that is also true regarding these new realities. Indeed, when women gather for social or other informal meetings, the conversations usually include discussions and comments on anticipated future changes. The closer we get to the last third of life, the more we seem to have targeted discussions that address the concerns of our older years. Many times, these concerns revolve around planning for retirement with anticipated changes in income, work roles, and health. We are concerned about whether we can adapt sufficiently. To help us adapt, we may have found resources offering solutions for future planning, and we share those resources with our friends. One book club friend said recently to one of the authors, "I am not sure if it is the blind leading the blind, but surely it is easier to share ideas and solutions than to fuss all by yourself."

This process of sharing concerns in small groups has been very useful for women in the past, and we are increasing the use of this process as we go forward. During the years of the women's movement, we called these groups "consciousness-raising groups"; now we call it "going to lunch."

## Reinvention as a Response to Transition

Uncertainty about the future is both exhilarating and frightening. For some, the present reality of their later years is not what they had anticipated and differs from that for which they had prepared. Health and finances, work and leisure, as well as new roles and anticipated losses are topics of great interest, along with the joys of looking forward with great anticipation to "finally getting to do what I want" and having the gift of free time.

A compilation of the responses of many of our interviewees shows a generally invigorated attitude. Our interviewees were successful and inventive as young women, and they continue to be generative and inventive as they grow older. These women have been able to modify their behaviors and attitudes as they age and have also been able to find solutions to difficult situations without growing negative and dissatisfied. In short, they are aging positively, for the most part, and now they are giving back to the generations behind them.

This is not to say that women don't have concerns about the next phase of their lives. They clearly do. But one theme keeps appearing: older women are using pieces of their life puzzles and all that they have gathered along the way to address the issues of the upcoming, unknown phase of their lives. They have also become resources to other women and have richly shared their ideas, strategies, and energies. They embrace new roles, they build new networks, they nurture new ideas, they have strengths to create and renew, they have creativity to invent and reinvent, they have the determination to succeed, and they have the will to do it. They have become skilled in making transitions, and their older years are just one more of life's continual and cyclical transitions.

*** 

The following chapters will detail many of the adventures and experiences that forty American women over the age of sixty have had and will reveal more about the reinventions and the dreams that are guiding their futures.

# CHAPTER 3

# Changing Roles, Responsibilities, and Relationships

## So, what am I going to be when I grow up?

## Growing up with Gender Stereotypes

Early in the first third of life, often by age three, people begin to ask children, "What do you want to be when you grow up?" The women born in the early part of the twentieth century might have looked around at their playthings and seen their dolls, stuffed animals, tea sets, play kitchens, and maybe a dollhouse. They often answered the question with some version of "a mommy." If their mother had a profession, they might have added teacher, nurse, secretary, or some descriptor of the limited number of jobs women did outside the home. Little boys, on the other hand, were most likely to have trucks, cars, fire engines, building blocks, or erector sets in their toy boxes. There's a small chance that their answers might have been "a daddy," but it is more likely that they would have named an occupation such as fireman, policeman, doctor, soldier, or some other predominantly male job. Today, as various career paths have become less gender specific and more women work outside the home, we find that both boys and girls are playing with similar toys. Still, it is mostly the girls who "play house" and the boys who "play trucks."

Our first inclination in life is to be just like our same-sex parent. We identify with Mommy or Daddy very strongly and begin to imitate their behaviors, dress, and mannerisms. Since the women's movement of the 1960s, many parents have made a concerted effort to expose both their sons and daughters to non-stereotypical toys and activities in order to even the playing field and present nonsexist role models to their children. Additionally, in recent years enlightened parents have gone out of their way to present a broad array of role models to their daughters to convey that they can be anything they want to be and do not have to be confined to traditionally female roles and careers. Today, most parents and teachers are aware of the influences that playthings, books, role models, and various language patterns have on children, and they select these items and activities with more awareness of their impact.

How gender roles evolve is not yet clearly understood. The prevalent view is that gender roles are determined by our physiology and that they also have a psychological component. We view childhood as a time when gender roles are laid down. During puberty, various gender role possibilities begin to emerge, and most pubescent boys and girls become aware that they have choices about how they present themselves and behave. These are the years when identity formation is the priority issue for both males and females.

The most obvious outward manifestation of gender is dress. Although there are now unisex hair styles and informal attire, such as jeans, each boy and girl begins to make choices that solidify their gender identity. One's appearance plays a key role in the identity struggles of adolescence.

It is during the adolescent years that questions about career choices begin to be asked. There are discussions about what courses to take and what studies are available in schools to prepare one for various careers. Even one's choice of school reflects one's interests. We now have schools that focus on art, and others that are strong in science. We have courses that prepare kids for college and those that prepare kids for jobs. As these school-based decisions are made, our views of gender appropriateness become apparent once again. Is it okay for a girl to become an engineer? Can a boy become a nurse? As each family answers these questions with their children, the shape of the future begins to emerge.

## Parental Impact on Gender Roles

Our interviewees often spoke of the limits of their choices as young women. Asked about early work and educational experiences, they offered insights such as, "My parents did not think higher education was for girls" or "There weren't as many choices for girls in the work-force when I was growing up." Yet this was by no means a universal experience among them. One seventy-two-year-old woman who had had an illustrious career in journalism and art said, "My formal edu-cation began late, after I worked as a secretary [at] a newspaper. As I learned how the business worked, I was promoted to more and more responsible positions from within. When it became important that I have a degree in order to climb the next rung, I had both encour-agement and financial support from my employer to go to college. I finished night school at the age of forty with a BA in design." Others commented that it had been their parents who had made sure that they went to college so that they could have better career choices. Often they were among the first women in their field or had created new job titles and roles for themselves during their working years. They enjoyed their careers and were either still working at them with no immediate plans to retire or had used their past careers to continue to be involved in the workforce as consultants, mentors, and community volunteers.

## Basic Questions

In young adulthood, we lay the groundwork for the rest of our lives in terms of roles and responsibilities. No matter what are our particular choices and decisions, three recurring internal life questions are posed: Who am I? To what groups do I belong? How do I function? Throughout our lives, we repeatedly ask ourselves and answer these three questions as we choose our partners and friends, select our careers, decide our religious affiliations, join political parties, elect candidates, generate the patterns of our daily lives, and make long-term commitments.

While we usually set the pace for future years during young adult-hood, somewhere between ages eighteen and thirty, these same ques-tions are posed again and again as we navigate the next phase of life, from ages thirty to sixty. We might stay on the first life course we select: stay married to the same person, elect a major in college that prepares us for a career in which we spend our entire work lives, and build our home in the same community where we grew up, then continue to live there. Or we might shift gears at various transition points: marry and divorce more than once, change majors in college, change not only jobs but careers at a number of junctures, and frequently move around the country or even the world. Whichever kind of lifestyle we embark upon, the three life questions must be asked and answered repeatedly, whether or not we are conscious of doing so. We found our interviewees to be consciously aware of these questions, for when asked what the future held for them, many of our interviewees would quip with a smile, "You mean, what am I going to do when I grow up?"

## Juggling Family and Work in Midlife

The second third of life, from age thirty to age sixty, is often referred to as midlife, with all of its attendant decisions, crises, and accomplishments. During this period we are usually at our prime while we establish ourselves as professionals or employees, raise our families, build financial stability, and try to maintain our good health and well-being. These are the years to make it, to feather our nests, find success, and become a respected and contributing member of the community. These are socially and materially productive adult years.

For some women, this second phase of life brings the necessary resolution of issues regarding work and family. As females settle into careers, they often wrestle with issues related to work and child rearing. Some women feel that they must catch up if they have taken time out of the workforce while their children are young. Women who have continued to work while raising their families have been doing two full-time jobs simultaneously. They find that as they are relieved of part of their at-home job when their children are grown and move out on their own, new opportunities arise. With new opportunities, some begin new careers, often in fields that didn't exist or were not available to them earlier, or decide to get further education, perhaps finishing studies they gave up when their children were young, feeling that now it's their turn. During this period there is often a sense of increased freedom. Women discover more ways to grow and develop their own talents and interests. Some of the negative aspects of the empty nest syndrome are often offset as they explore a world teeming with possibilities. They take on the roles of adult friends to those younger than they are and watch their children, nieces, nephews, and grandchildren grow and adapt to the demands and new opportunities in their particular generation. If they are able, they may financially contribute to the educational goals of the younger generations or act as mentors to them. Some take over responsibilities of rearing their grandchildren in circumstances where parents cannot continue to do so. But mainly, women find that by the end of the second third of their lives, they have time to devote to their own interests, and they are excited, grateful, and pleased about it. Said one of our interviewees, a former administrator, "My new role is not being so busy. I decide every day what to do."

## Caregiving and Sandwiching

During the second third, some women experience serious illness: their own, their parents', their spouse's, and, in some cases, their children's. Women continue to be the major caregivers of ill or disabled family members, and these circumstances severely limit the choices that women have, today as in the past. If their spouse becomes incapacitated and they are left as the only breadwinner, then work becomes a necessity and must be sufficient enough to provide for whatever dependents there are, in addition to self-support. If a spouse dies, the widow may be left with large financial and other burdens that color every aspect of her life. The financial circumstances of a widow's life will usually determine what choices she can and cannot make in the future.

People in their second third must also often start caring for their parents as well as their nuclear family members. The financial burden and increased responsibilities that occur when parents become frail and need help can be devastating to a family already juggling at-home children, children in college, or adult children on the brink of becoming new parents themselves. The stresses of being in between two or more generations as the main provider can break apart some of the strongest families. The label "sandwich generation" was meant to be a light-hearted way to describe the position in which people find themselves when this happens. But increasingly it has become a way to express the feelings that accompany the changes required to manage the situation.

The group participants who met weekly in Florida often discussed being "sandwiched" and how to cope with it. Many had found their late second third and much of their third third occupied by caring for more than one generation at a time. Although many had accepted the roles in which they were needed, they often expressed frustration about the physical, financial, and mental worries that were brought about at a time during which they had planned to be free of dependents, in good health, and enjoying themselves. "I'm squashed between layers," one stated. Undoubtedly, the challenges that face women in their older years as caregivers can affect their vitality and their health, as well as their financial well-being.

## Midlife Marital Crises and Changes

During the middle adult years some marriages begin to feel stale, and companionship with the opposite sex may be sought outside the marriage. If these extramarital relationships become satisfying and serious, separation or divorce may become an option. While women may be becoming more assertive and self-confident at this time of their lives, and thus more prone to seeking out new romantic relationships, men may also see themselves as more loving and desirable and seek new affiliations and relationships with women other than their own spouses.

On the other hand, some marriages may grow closer as the hectic pace of family responsibilities slows and there are quiet times of togetherness that were the cornerstone of a younger marriage. Words used by our interviewees to describe this type of marital regrowth were "best partners again," "rediscovered happiness," "learning to be more in love than before," and "being in tune to the couple we were before the kids." The busy early midlife years definitely test marital and other relationships. But each decade can also introduce new joys and enhance our relationships as we get older.

It can't be denied that there are critical turning points in our second third. Navigating modern life successfully through these demanding years requires stamina, perseverance, balance, and maturity. Those who recognize that this is a time of change and upheaval that can test the most secure relationships can find new doors to open and gain assurance that the investments they have made in marriage can be maintained throughout the remaining years.

## Facing the Future Decades

At age fifty, we become aware that we have already lived through our own personal half century and that there are more years behind us than in front of us. At this point, if one is not content, radical decisions may be made: leaving the family, starting a new intimate relationship, quitting a job, going off to paint on a beach somewhere, or going into therapy to discover what is causing a major sense of dissatisfaction. Women as well as men may feel like they have only a short time left to fulfill their dreams and live the kind of life they really want to live. Some women may feel trapped and unable to extricate themselves from their current situation, especially if they are financially dependent on a spouse. Some women look to change their physical appearance, seeking to recapture their youth; others begin to travel with women friends or go to a spa to rejuvenate themselves; still others feel that they have few options but to stay with their situation no matter how unsatisfactory. Some believe that being older is a sign of honor. One grandmother said, "It isn't how many wrinkles you have, it is whether when you smile, they all go up!" It may be that rejuvenating oneself is just stopping long enough to appreciate what you are now, being joyous in having another day to be in the world, and passing on what you have learned over many years. Most of our interviewees were very comfortable in their skins…no matter how wrinkled.

## Networking and New Relationships

Between ages thirty and sixty, there is ample time to pursue and develop new relationships, with both women and men. Social and networking skills are especially useful if women are recovering from the loss of a spouse. Bereavement groups and divorcees' groups are often helpful in forming new friendships and relationships with others in the same boat. Sometimes new romances are born in these support groups, when widows and widowers or those who have been divorced begin to share their new status and find each other comforting and companionable.

Women who have been single well into their fifties may have an advantage in this situation, in contrast to widows or divorcees: they are accustomed to being financially independent and have usually established social networks and habits that are satisfactory for them. If they are single but wish to find a partner and marry, the habits of their first third give way to new ways of establishing relationships. But as the years progress, it becomes increasingly difficult to find a compatible partner.

When previous marriages and children are part of the equation, the independence of singlehood sometimes becomes difficult to trade for the complexities of marriage, stepchildren, and other new family relationships. Because of the many legal, financial, and emotional complexities of second and perhaps third marriages, it has become increasingly common for women and men to decide to live together without marrying when they want to share their lives during the second and third thirds. This phenomenon is a significant shift of cultural norms. These arrangements are increasingly being accepted in American society and present many challenges for which there are few role models. One widowed interviewee said, "Neither nurse nor purse for me!" as she explained why she would not marry again. A divorced woman who had been in a relationship with a man for a number of years put it this way, "No, I don't want to get married again. I want more freedom now. I enjoy my free time and would like to spend more time with my women friends."

Given women's career patterns today, an increasing number of women wait until their thirties to marry and have children in their thirties and forties, beginning their family lives in their second third. Today's lengthening life spans and extensive fertility options allow many women to wait until their midlife years to begin a family. Each decade pushes on the next so that today, many women are well into their sixties before their children are grown and leave home. These changing circumstances affect not only one's current decade, but all those that follow. It is often said that "today's fifty is yesterday's forty," which usually means that even though the big five-o has arrived, the person still feels young and in their midlife period. Subsequently, if "today's sixty is yesterday's fifty," we are not really "old" at sixty, but are still in our midlife years. If this is so, the next third-third group, who are now women in their fifties, will differ once again from those of us in our third third now. We of the Greatest Generation[1] might be able to listen to the needs of those women just one decade younger than we are, the baby boomers, and help them to make good transitions into their sixties and seventies. It might surprise and please them that the years ahead are not necessarily going to be elderly years, but can be interesting, active, mature, and energetic years. One of the most effective ways to learn this is for boomers to network with Greatest Generation women and reach out for new friendships and relationships with women just a few years older than they are.

## What Our Over-Sixty Interviewees Said

The first questions we asked our interviewees were, "Because women are veteran multitaskers, both by training and disposition, what do you see as the multiple roles of your present age? How are the roles you now have different from before?"

Regardless of their age, our interviewees defined their roles and responsibilities in terms of the others in their lives. Those with husbands, partners, or parents who were ill, disabled, or institutionalized told us about their caretaker roles. One husband had heart problems, another was in a nursing home for patients with Alzheimer's disease. One was legally blind, one had suffered a stroke, another had multiple health problems and generalized weakness, and still another had developed back problems. In all these instances, our female interviewee was relatively healthy in comparison to her spouse and the activities of her entire day were defined by her relatively dependent male partner. If her partner was confined largely to their home or to an institutional setting, a great deal of daily time was spent at medical appointments or visiting the confined partner. The woman's freedom was severely limited, and the role of caretaker took priority over other aspects of her life. Even so, one interviewee put a positive spin on her caretaker role: "My husband's bypass was an opportunity of a lifetime. We've gotten much closer...I'm grateful I can do it."

Those interviewees who were divorced, widowed, or had remained single and were living essentially alone felt an enormous sense of freedom. Some had acquired a new boyfriend, and a few were sharing their homes with an unmarried adult child or a female friend. Rather than expressing loneliness, they had shifted gears into their single selves and were taking on roles from other stages of their lives. Those who had enjoyed learning and had been good students in earlier years had returned to a pursuit of learning and were taking courses, reading voraciously, and participating in book groups or other discussion groups. They had recaptured their roles as students and were feeling very successful and stimulated. They gravitated toward women friends who were alert and well-informed, became involved in politics and community causes, and had a real sense of well-being.

About a third of the interviewees were married, healthy, and had relatively healthy spouses. These women expressed satisfaction that they were spending quality time with their spouses traveling, going out to dinner, attending concerts and theater performances, spending time outdoors, and generally enjoying the rich and stimulating time they were having with their partners. They were grateful for their good health, and many of them were conscientiously exercising and trying to remain in good condition.

Everyone took great pleasure in their adult children and especially in their grandchildren. A few had great-grandchildren. One of the eldest women from our study group, who has eleven grandchildren and twenty-three great-grandchildren, described these years as "the harvest of life," a time filled with family celebrations and reunions. She said, "I support them all...whatever makes them happy." Another felt that this period of her life was "the payoff" for all her prior investments in her family and her work.

A genuine sense of pride and plain joy were expressed when grandchildren were described. All our interviewees had many photographs of their family in their homes and were eager to show them to us, accompanied by elaborate efforts to name every person in the pictures. This was a bit surprising, since all the women we interviewed had been working women, at least at some time in their lives, and were not focused only on their roles as mothers and grandmothers. Even so, at this stage in their lives there was a universal sense of accomplishment and pleasure relative to their family roles. Those who did not have children of their own spoke of their nieces and nephews. It was clear that these women's lives, too, were greatly enriched by their family relationships. And the pure joy of having grandchildren and great-grandchildren was expressed universally, accompanied by broad smiles and proud anecdotes.

In a few instances, we encountered women who had disabled adult children. Clearly, these women continued to feel responsible for their offspring and worried about what might become of them after they themselves died. The housing, financial situations, and care of these dependent adult children who were not able to care for themselves remains a significant unaddressed problem in our society. There are few societal support systems for these circumstances. For the most part, legislators have not adequately addressed these issues, states have not developed clear and comprehensive policies or a sufficient number of facilities to care for developmentally disabled adults, and many women are left to seek out resources by themselves. There are no good solutions, and the costs to each individual family are immense as they try to provide health insurance, life insurance, safe housing, and personal care for their disabled adult children. These circumstances severely limit these mothers' decisions. Difficulties are compounded if the father is not available as the result of divorce or death. Then the aging mother may be the sole supporter of the disabled adult child during a time when she herself needs additional care. A number of new roles and relationships between parent and child begin to gel during the third phase of a woman's life. As grown children go off on their own, they also become companions to their parents. Sometimes the parent-child roles are reversed: "My children tell me what to do, but I do things my way. I don't take orders," remarked one very independent interviewee. Another confessed, "We've reversed roles: my son is teaching me how to use the computer; my daughter takes me to the doctor."

Relationships deepen as our children become parents and want to share the ups and downs of their own children with us. If our children live nearby, daily interactions are facilitated and our roles as grandparents take on a priority in the course of our daily lives. We become babysitters, homework assistants, and football game companions. These are usually welcome new roles. Some of us may even become full-time nannies when our daughters and daughters-in-law return to work. When this occurs, our own third-third plans may go on hold as we, once again, become full-time caregivers.

When our grown children and their children live far away, most of us spend a great deal of time and money traveling to see them to try to ensure that we are part of their young lives. One of our interviewees, who had a long-term blended marriage, had five adult children and stepchildren. All lived out of town except one. All had children of their own; a few were divorced and lived in different cities from their children, the interviewee's grandchildren. This woman and her husband had made a commitment to see all five of their children and their eight grandchildren at least twice each year. This travel schedule was a challenge and occupied a large chunk of their time as well as their funds. Yet the interviewee loved every minute of the constant pace. "Oh," she said with a warm smile, "what could be more wonderful than spending time with my grandchildren? We are so lucky!"

There is universal delight in our grandchildren, and a special joy comes to women as they embrace their grandchildren in an environment relatively free from the need to discipline them. Grandchildren represent the best of our intergenerational relationships and learning. "There is nothing like it!" she purred, referring to becoming a grandparent.

## Enduring Friendships

Some of the most important kinds of relationships during the third third of our lives are our friendships with other women. Women often develop informal social groups during these years, similar to the typically female slumber parties, sororities, and women's organizations of their youth. Only now we may have golf buddies, bridge partners, travel companions, adult education study partners, former work colleagues with whom we have lunch, and book club friends. There is more time to get together as we decrease our work and other commitments. While some women are extending themselves to acquire new friends, others are solidifying their friendships and have fewer, but closer, friends. In either case, women are seeking deeper, more meaningful relationships in their later years. "Now that I'm not working so much anymore, I'm making more time for my friends," said one interviewee. Another confided, "I don't have time for negative people. I only have finite time, and I must decide how to spend it on positive people and activities."

Women's networks also fill important roles during these later years as we become more interdependent with other women, especially if husbands have died or are infirm. But regardless of the health of our partners, we women seem to make time for our networks of women friends. We maintain our memberships in professional organizations just to stay in touch and keep up with our career fields. In truth, we cherish our relationships and professional networks. Some of us continue to serve on nonprofit organization boards to not only give back to our communities, but to stay in the fray and continue to develop new, meaningful relationships. Most of us don't want to give up our relationships and volunteer networks, even as others are ready to be replaced by younger volunteers and be free to move to retirement communities and travel. Some of us still pay exorbitant dues in order to remain on mailing lists and continue to be included in activities, programs, and luncheons. In truth, we yearn for the human connections with old friends and new acquaintances. *Networking* is a contemporary word for *quilting circle* or *sewing circle*. In all ages, women have gathered together to share work or hobbies. In many instances these activities were merely excuses for making time and space to visit together and nurture our friendships and networks.

During the third third of life, we often reach back in time to the friends of our youth. Surprisingly, the phone rings and an old high school friend is calling. Former boyfriends begin to show up again. High school and college reunions spark both old and new relationships. Sometimes former romances blossom after many years of separation and the deaths of spouses. It is not uncommon to hear a woman say, "We began to talk just like we used to, as if we had seen each other every day, when in fact we haven't seen each other for fifty years!"

Perhaps because we are engaging in mental life reviews, we seem to be open to reaching back into our pasts and former lives to recapture friendships and relationships that were left dormant for many years. There is comfort in being with people who shared an earlier stage of our lives. And there is a need in all of us for continuity in the midst of change and for the security that the relationships of our youth represent.

This third of our life is a time in which we separate the important from the trivial. There is simply not enough time left to waste a single day. Our roles and relationships, therefore, are with the people we most care about. At this point in life, we are clearer about who is important to us and with whom we want to spend our limited time. These increasingly scarce hours are going to be spent with those who matter to us most. We are coming to terms with our own mortality and we jealously guard our precious though limited time. We are finally realizing which roles we want to play and in which relationships we want to invest.

## Four Patterns

As we examined the changing roles and relationships in this third of women's lives, four distinct patterns emerged. First, there was the predominant caretaker role with its attendant responsibilities. The daily lives of these caretaker women were largely defined by others' needs and their responsibilities to be on call day and night for the sake of another person, usually a spouse in ill health. These women had little choice; their roles were a function of lifelong devotions and loyalties. They did not express outright resentment, although they acknowledged that their situations were not what they would have chosen. It is not uncommon for caregivers to feel both sadness and exhaustion, even in the face of their steadfast dedication to the situation. When asked once, they deny it. Asked a second time, in a different way, and they may tell about their individual problems in this situation and how they wish it were different. But in spite of their sense of duty, most led full and active lives that transcended the dependencies of their mates.

The second pattern was one of interdependence, which was evident for more than half of the interviewees. For the most part, these were married women whose lives were still intertwined with their husbands or significant others. Most of them were working, participating in active social lives, relatively healthy, and engaged in a variety of community activities. Their roles and relationships had not changed measurably as they transitioned from their second thirds to their third thirds. The biggest change was usually that grandchildren had been added to their multiple roles, and this was a very welcome addition that influenced how they spent their nonworking time and where they traveled.

These women were beginning to trim the time that they spent on previous community and work activities as they transitioned into their third thirds. They were beginning to be selfish with their limited days and were making decisions about the balance of work and leisure in their lives. They had lived long enough and had enough experience to know how they wanted to enjoy life to its fullest while they were healthy. And they were now confident enough to put their plans into action. Some were consciously preparing for retirement, others were phasing into retirement, and still others had made the transition out of employment and were now focusing their energies on those relationships and activities that were the most meaningful to them.

The third pattern was dependence. Those few interviewees who were quite dependent on others had serious illnesses: Parkinson's disease, heart failure, and cancer. These circumstances demanded a greater dependence on others than these women were accustomed to. Because they had been vigorous and energetic, independent people prior to this episode in their lives, they continued to be creative with their time and energies, limited as these resources had become. Yet their illnesses defined much of what they did each day. "This disease has sapped my energy. And it's boring. That's what illness does to a person," said one interviewee.

When treatment was the priority, others cared for them. When medications were needed, others brought their medicines to them. Still, even in their dependent roles, they valued their close friendships, participated in community activities as best they could, read a great deal, and remained upbeat in their attitudes. "They tell me I've done some wonderful things in my life and I should rest on my laurels. But I miss the creativity. Besides, what am I going to do with my box of awards and certificates?" asked one publicly known woman who has a progressive illness. Even in her discomfort she was volunteering for an oral history project where she was able to interview older people and record their stories for the local museum.

Another person asked, "Have you ever been dependent on anyone or others to do what your brain tells you that you ought to be able to do, but your body doesn't respond? It is one of the most frustrating state of affairs to ever be in, and there is nothing I could do about it." Even making changes to her lifestyle and accepting help had not made this frustration any more acceptable over the several years she had been partially disabled. She was still very active, but she fought with depression, anger, and futility about her circumstances. Still, she was a busy person trying to cope with this situation. She said, "Most people think I am wonderful. I smile, I love other people, and when I can, I help. But never knowing what day I can't function is really awful."

Because being dependent was not their past normal state, it was difficult to ameliorate their fears or frustration. The best thing was for their loved ones to remain alert to their ups and downs and maintain a presence in their lives. Yet these women remained very stressed. One said, "My illness is a pervasive issue. It affects all aspects of my life." These previously fiercely independent women, now dependent on children, spouses, relatives, and friends, had tried to learn new physical habits and they had became role models of bravery, strength, and perseverance for their children and grandchildren, even as they grow increasingly dependent on those around them. Should those on whom they depend disappear from their lives, serious choices about housing, daily chores, medical care, and finances would become priorities. For those women with adult children, there are close family members upon whom they can depend. For the single women or those without family nearby, another phase of new roles and relationships will begin.

The fourth pattern of new emerging roles and relationships during the sixty-plus years of life is independence. Almost half of our interviewees were, indeed, independent. And there were different levels and types of independence. The women who had never been married, were divorced, or had been widowed were independent in terms of daily living and financial matters. About 10 percent of our interviewees were living in this situation. Their roles included financial self-support, in some cases through continued work; independent housing; continuing activities in the community; and the complete assumption of responsibility for their own well-being and social life. There are a number of remarkable qualities about these women. They remain optimistic and upbeat in spite of significant losses. They have learned to live alone. They have assumed all their own financial responsibilities. They make their own investment decisions or choose a professional for this task. They travel alone or invite women friends to go on trips with them. They enroll in courses and continue to seek new learning. They learn to live with silence. They have a complete sense of freedom in their aloneness, while accepting the ultimate responsibilities for their own lives and well-being. Whether by choice or circumstance, they must "make it" on their own. They are, indeed, to be admired and respected for their perseverance and strength.

In the third third of life, many of us will experience this self-reliant situation, although not always of our own choosing. Rapidly increasing longevity predicts that this will be so. These independent women are the role models for us. They deserve our attention and admiration. In the not too distant future, the population of single, self-reliant women in their sixties, seventies, eighties, and nineties will explode. We would be well advised to pay careful attention to how our female friends and relatives negotiate the challenges of independence during these years of their lives.

## A Few Words on Religion and Spirituality

Although the conventional wisdom is that in our later years we turn to God and our religious heritage for comfort and solace, this was not the case for most of our interviewees. In reality, two-thirds of our interviewees expressed dissatisfaction with the formal religious institutions of their childhood. Most were not regular churchgoers and did not perform those at-home rituals they had been taught. Only one-third were members of a congregation and were actively engaged with their church or synagogue. Of those, a few held religion and faith as central to their lives, and they were avid practitioners and participants. On the other hand, a few were members of a congregation but were not actively involved. Of those involved more formally in a religious institution, some were explicitly critical of their own religious leaders and their roles in the world, including their denomination's official positions on politics, women's issues, and matters of personal choice. However, most of our interviewees were very interested in spirituality and belief systems. They had explored many faiths and cultures and were, for the most part, eclectic and accepting of a wide variety of beliefs, both within their families and their communities.

Intermarriage between their children and men or women of a different faith was surprisingly common. This caused our interviewees' understanding and appreciation of faiths different from their own to grow. Many families celebrated both Christmas and Channukah or holidays of other faiths important to the younger family. Buddhism occupied a position of philosophical interest for many of our interviewees. By and large, these women in their third-third decades were reflective, introspective, and sincere in their spiritual searching. In

46

sum, it could be said that for these women religious differences were not only tolerated, but were appreciated and embraced.

Our interviewee group included women raised in a variety of Catholic, Protestant, and Jewish traditions. All had examined their religious faiths and practices throughout their lives and come to some accommodations that were comfortable for them and for their families. While one reflective woman advised, "Trust the unfolding," another quipped "If I had a choice, I'd be a Jewish Quaker!"

One woman who was a professional minister explained, "Lots of people turn their backs on religion in their older years, while others long to be connected with something other than self." Now, in the last third of their lives, most of our interviewees knew how and what to preserve and what to discard relative to their faiths and their spiritual lives. They did not appear to be in quandaries about what they believed but rather had already come to grips with their relationships, their traditions, and their beliefs and were comfortable with the role that religion did or did not play on their lives. One does not know how these patterns of belief and ritual will be maintained or will change, especially as various health issues emerge and matters of death and dying take front and center in their lives. But for now, a sense of calm prevails.

Many of our interviewees expressed less of a need for formal religion than for a more spiritual life. They said things such as, "I'm on a new spiritual path, but formal religion plays a lesser role" and "I meditate every day and read spiritual stuff." In contrast, another said, "My religion is central to my life. I'm very connected." No one formula fit all.

# CHAPTER 4

# Women and Work

**Man may work from sun to sun,
but woman's work is never done.**
—Old saying

"Women's work," as mentioned in the old adage, typically relates to the home and family: giving birth to and caring for children, managing the family's activities, getting and preparing food, acquiring and taking care of clothing, decorating and maintaining the interior of the home, gardening and caring for the exterior of the home, providing for children's schooling and after-school activities, car pooling, planning family entertainment and travel, arranging for events such as weddings and funerals, and ensuring the family's health and care at times of illness.

No matter if a woman is single or married, in a relationship, or if she has children, she is usually responsible for the domestic side of life. Though some husbands have assumed some responsibility for the household scene in recent years, most domestic work remains "women's work."

As we all know, women are also the ones who become pregnant, give birth to babies, breast feed them, and, due to these circumstances, are the primary caregivers during a child's infancy. Nannies may help, housekeepers may help, cooks may help, gardeners may help, and husbands may help. But, raised by mothers whose identities were mostly defined by their domestic skills, most of the women we interviewed have always done and continue to do the lion's share of domestic work in the home.

## Is Our Nest Ever Going to Be Empty?

Even into the later years, after age sixty, most women must either perform the domestic tasks of their household, enlist their spouse or partner to share those tasks, or pay someone else to do them. Women are still the primary home managers, even when they are not full-time, always-on-the-scene housewives.

By the time the women are in their sixth decade, most of their children have grown up, moved out of the home, and are functioning on their own. If this is the case, the parents they leave behind are called "empty nesters." But if parents have failed at getting their children ready for independence, many of those adult children move back home. We are now seeing many grown adult children, even beyond age thirty, returning to their childhood homes. When this happens, and whether we like it or not, it is usually the mother who again provides the domestic environment and performs the domestic tasks that support these "recycled" adult children. While fathers might fuss about the financial aspects of these renewed dependencies, mothers often continue to perform daily household tasks on behalf of their children—usually in addition to attending to their spouses' needs—in this unexpected arrangement. It is not surprising that women do this, even though these interruptions in the usual course of adult development may need to be suppressed and children moved out of the "nest" into their adult environments. Yet younger mothers who are now forty or fifty commonly accept this situation. Their upbringing and training may have reinforced the notion that mothers are always responsible for the welfare of their children, and they have not yet found a way to wrestle with the problem of requiring adult children to become responsible for their own lives.

Our interviewees were not so sanguine about supporting adult children who have come back home. As young women, they were expected to leave home after adolescence, attend college or become employed, marry, and wrestle with their own independent lives. They are confounded by this growing tendency in their daughters' and sons' families. One eloquent seventy-year-old woman who had left home at age eighteen to pursue her own life mused that she had worked since she was a child and was both taught and expected to add to the family's growth to the best of her ability until she finished her high school education. At that time, she understood that she needed to find the means to create a life of continued learning and development. So she entered the armed services, where food, clothing, and training were part of what her independent life offered. Her parents continued to support her efforts with enthusiasm, pride, and pleasure, as well as with small tokens of financial support when they could. But they made it clear that unless tragedy struck, coming home to live was not an option. For our interviewee, meeting these expectations was a source of pride and motivation. The independence she gained from her parents was a benefit to her all her life. "I went to Chicago when I was eighteen," she reported, "and lived with my sister while I went to school. Then I bought a business in Nebraska for $640 and paid it off at $50 a month. When World War II started, I enlisted and became a WAVE. We 'girls' were dental assistants in the US Navy. After the war, I went back to my business and got married." This woman had made it on her own and helped her parents for many years. That was simply what was expected.

## Women, the Workplace, and Pregnancy Issues

As the patterns of women's lives continue to evolve and career commitments and choices cause women to have children later in life, domestic circumstances are changing dramatically. This now relatively common reality puts our society in yet-to-be charted waters regarding how women will be affected throughout their life cycle based on their reproductive choices. Just as the second third of women's life is changing, the third portion of women's lives will look different when the next generation of women reaches age sixty and beyond, especially relative to their roles as mothers and homemakers.

Over the past half century, advances in women's health, reproductive technology, and gynecological care have provided contemporary women with expanding birth control methods and family planning devices so that women today are able to plan when and if to have children.

And as further advances in procedures such as in vitro fertilizations, egg and embryo transplants, and sperm donations have become more accessible, effective, and affordable, more women have been able to bear children well into their forties. Occasionally, we read about a woman becoming a mother, sometimes for the first time, in her fifties or sixties. These situations are still fairly uncommon, but there are those who now consider a woman's age irrelevant to the question of whether or not she could or should have children or remain at work. Others insist that women should stick to the traditional child-bearing ages, which by convention used to end at around age forty. At the present time, although it is still statistically true that women between twenty and forty have the healthiest pregnancies and births, we are steadily gathering both information about forty-plus mothers having their first babies as well as the experience and technology to deal with difficulties, should they arise. Thus it is becoming more common to see women in their forties accompanying their toddlers to preschool. Many of these women had successful careers for more than twenty years before they began a family.

It is clearly not the same situation for a man. There are daily examples of men becoming new fathers in their fifties, sixties, and even seventies. And these occasions are celebrated. Think about the celebrity men who have had children with much younger mates: Larry King, Donald Trump, Hugh Hefner, Clint Eastwood, and Charlie Chaplin, to name just a few. This is one of the fundamental differences between men and women: the age at which we can become parents and perform the work of child rearing.

These issues of pregnancy and child rearing are essential in a discussion of women at work, because the demands of being a parent and homemaker are intertwined with work throughout a woman's adult years. The relationship between work and domestic roles has a different impact on women than it does on men.

For women, it is important to view the entire life cycle in a uniquely feminine way. Otherwise, we will not be able to really appreciate and understand both the life cycles and work issues in the lives of both men and women. Although there are some similarities, they are not the same. There are other issues that we will also explore as we consider what women's work is, when they should do it, and when they should stop.

## The Women's Movement

When Betty Friedan wrote *The Feminine Mystique* in 1963, her first chapter described the now-famous "problem that has no name."

> The problem lay buried, unspoken, for many years in the minds of American women. It was a strange stirring, a sense of dissatisfaction, a yearning that women suffered in the middle of the twentieth century in the United States. Each suburban wife struggled with it alone. As she made the beds, shopped for groceries, matched slipcover material, ate peanut butter sandwiches with her children, chauffeured Cub Scouts and Brownies, lay beside her husband at night—she was afraid to ask even of herself the silent question—"Is this all?"[1]

Friedan continued to describe the unnamed condition and then concluded her first chapter as follows:

> If I am right, the problem that has no name stirring in the minds of so many women today is not a loss of femininity or too much education or the demands of domesticity. It is far more important than anyone recognizes. It is the key to these other new and old problems which have been torturing women and their husbands and children, and puzzling their doctors and educators for years. It may well be the key to our future as a nation and a culture. We can no longer ignore that voice within women that says: "I want something more than my husband and my children and my home."[2]

Thus began the period of time in our history that we now refer to as the women's movement. Historians call the second wave of the women's movement the period of time from 1963 to 1975 and view the first wave as the struggle for women's right to vote, which began in 1848 and culminated in 1920.[3] Although women in their third phase of life today recall the women's movement of the 1960s and 1970s in a variety of ways, there can be little doubt that Friedan was right about one thing: the events of those years changed women's lives dramatically. And those changes have indeed altered our nation and our culture forever, as Friedan quite accurately predicted. One recent well-crafted summary of those changes, documented in a reference book of feminist biographies, follows:

> The [2,220] biographies include feminists who shaped our revolution through theory; fought endlessly over decades for the Equal Rights Constitutional Amendment; fought for control over our own bodies; overcame discriminatory practices in pay and promotions; made it possible for pregnant women to keep their jobs; greatly increased job opportunities by integrating Help Wanted advertising; passed legislation to ensure that girls have access to sports, science and math programs; introduced new approaches to healthcare; experimented with non-hierarchical structures; formed health groups and health centers so that women's needs could be met in a woman-focused environment; introduced non-sexist language in children's textbooks; helped women obtain the right to their own property, their own credit, and use of their own names; fought for tax deductions for home and childcare expenses; established childcare centers; worked privately and publicly for partnership marriages with shared responsibilities; established women's studies and women's history programs so that women became a recognized and respected focus of study; changed the way women are regarded in areas of psychology, philosophy, politics, art and religion; addressed unfair treatment of women and children in poverty; established respectful treatment of rape victims and punishment of rapists. [...]

It was not only the concrete victories these feminists fought for and won—and sometimes did not win—that substantially changed women's lives; the culture[s] of our nation and the world were changed as well. And women themselves have changed. We are not the people we were before 1970. Women have come to expect full equality, and that is the greatest difference of all.[4]

During the twelve years of the second wave of the women's movement, today's sixty-year-old women were between sixteen and twenty-eight years of age. Today's seventy-year-olds were between twenty-six and thirty-eight years old, just beginning the second third of life, and today's eighty-year-olds were between thirty-six and forty-eight years old. Those women now in their nineties would have been between age forty-six and fifty-eight. Therefore, the majority of today's women who are now in the third third of their lives were in the generative portion of their lives, when the contemporary women's movement was at its height. Those were the years when most of our current third-third women would have finished school and were starting jobs and careers. They were also getting married or choosing partners and starting households of their own. They were becoming mothers and defining their roles as parents. They were assuming adult and community responsibilities. They were in the midst of one of the busiest times of their lives. Whether or not they were actively engaged in the women's movement per se, their lives as adult women were influenced significantly by what was happening all around them. And those who were deeply involved in the movement's social-change activities were not only responsible for some of the previously identified changes but were themselves personally changed by these activities.

Thus it is not surprising that both the activist women who were redefining all aspects of their lives during the women's movement as well as those less activist women whose adult lives were directly affected by the many changes that were occurring in the 1960s and 1970s are now redefining the current period of their own lives. Women over sixty today are, once again, at the forefront of profound social change. They are creating new models of behavior and thought, just as they did when they were younger. These kinds of periodic reexaminations have become habitual, something they have done all of their adult lives. They see themselves as innovators residing on the leading edge, challenging the status quo. This is especially true in the realm of women's work. One interviewee in her mid-eighties assessed the women's movement this way: "Women today don't realize what we did. Women are in all kinds of jobs and professions now, in medicine, law, business, and corporations. It wasn't always like that."

Today's women over sixty have proven that one can be a wife, mother, and successful career woman. They have demonstrated that there are an infinite number of options for women. A woman can complete her studies, even through a doctorate or professional law or medical degree, and still become a wife and mother. She can start her own business or rise through the ranks of a large corporation and still become a wife and mother. Women can earn more than their husbands and still stay married. Or they need not be married at all: a single woman can become a mother and be the primary breadwinner for her family. Women no longer must choose between having a family and working outside the home; they can do both. And they can vary the sequence of these genuinely full-time jobs so that they can be successful in both arenas. But that is not to say it is easy, nor has it ever been. Contemporary women are talented multitaskers, just as women before them were or learned to be. They have much to teach each other and their daughters, who will do the same in a different milieu.

For the most part, today's women over sixty grew up after World War II. The eldest of this third third actively participated in that war as young adults. The can-do spirit of the war years taught these women that they could do anything they set their minds to. Certainly a mix of the strong self-images built in the war years in combination with the determination of activists in the women's movement two decades later supported these women in their groundbreaking redefinitions of women's roles.

## Our Interviewees as Working Women

In scheduling our interviews, we were mindful of the fact that we were talking to women who had worked outside the home in various fields and who greatly valued their work. Some had become very successful and were leaders in their disciplines. All enjoyed the intellectual challenge their work provided, the income it generated, the pleasure of working with colleagues they liked, and the value of their work to their communities and their countries. Some were fortunate to have all four of these dimensions present in their work environments. Few disliked their work.

One retired career woman in her early sixties was not atypical in saying, "I never had a job I didn't care about, or worked with people I didn't care about." Another very committed interviewee was even more emphatic: "Nobody I know stops working. It's their contribution to the world, not just a job." Still another expressed it this way: "Work is what I've always done. It's the center of my life. I'm the breadwinner. Work is my love!"

A brief glimpse at the work lives of some of our interviewees reveals the wide variety of their work arenas: actress, audiologist, economist, math teacher, jewelry designer, minister, nonprofit organization administrator, university teacher, beautician, writer, yoga instructor, state government agency administrator, educator, nurse educator, nurse practitioner, psychologist, retail business owner, small business owner, artist, entrepreneur, journalist, university administrator, foundation chief executive officer, federal government agency administrator, university faculty member, fiction writer, and professional association director. Several had held multiple positions as they entered the workforce and found new avenues for their talents.

Nurses are good examples of the diverse possibilities of work that have emerged from a once very straightforward role. Nurses are the largest workforce in health care, and the vast majority of nurses continue to be female, with direct patient-care responsibilities. But now they also own health insurance companies, hospitals, and health care management companies in addition to holding their basic nursing licenses. They are scientists and researchers, as well as teachers and military personnel, many of senior rank. Many have left direct nursing care and created corporations with health care interests, and they are also journal editors and writers. Many are entrepreneurs in innovative fields of health care delivery. But most will tell you that they are essentially nurses who have used their basic management and people skills to advance into new fields.

But women in all work arenas, not just nursing, have grown in and outgrown their original chosen work areas or educational fields. They are good managers of life, and thus, they are balancing multiple roles and creating new ones.

## The Family-Work Equation

Of our forty interviewees, thirty-five managed to raise children and also work outside the home in very demanding and time-consuming jobs. (Five did not have children and three did not marry but were committed to an individual partner or a religious community.) Most of our interviewees had worked in a wide variety of jobs and settings, and the majority had changed careers, some many times. The "infinite sequences of women's lives" can be seen from these interviews: school, marriage, alternative lifestyles, motherhood, careers, and retirement all entered these women's lives at varying times; there was no set chronology.

One of the most significant results of the twentieth-century women's movement has been that American women have demonstrated their capacity to integrate both family and work into the rich mosaic of their individual lives. They have done this by using a wide variety of time sequences to work in a broad diversity of fields and professions, and have done so with remarkable skill and elegance. A true revolution has taken place during the last forty years. Yet this revolution is not yet fully understood, appreciated, or integrated into our society and its institutions. A social lag exists. Many of our organizations and institutions are still out of step with the realities of women's lives and needs, especially in regard to work and its counterpart, retirement.

## Retirement

One of the most challenging and important aspects of our interviews was this complex issue of retirement. One woman in her early sixties who is self-employed put it this way: "The concept of retirement doesn't apply to women. I'm going to keep on doing what I do until I'm incompetent. I'll work as long as I can." Another reinforced that view: "I'll work as long as I can function. I'm not going to retire." In her mid-eighties, one businesswoman said, "Retirement doesn't exist. It has no meaning for me." "I don't see myself retiring," stated another. "It will be a new phase of my work."

It is becoming clear that the concept of retirement itself is primarily a male notion. Few women have worked in a continuous and linear fashion for only one employer throughout their lives. Most women have interrupted their work trajectories for various lengths of time to give birth and rear children, care for elderly parents or sick relatives, or return to school for advanced training or degrees. We call these patterns "stopping out." Although often falsely interpreted as "dropping out"—of school, community activities, or the workforce—women know among themselves that different priorities at different times of their lives require readjusting their schedules and changing how they deploy their energies. This process also has been called "shifting gears" or "transitioning."

Because of the cyclical nature of women's lives and their "stopping out" patterns, their perception of retirement is affected. Many women feel as though they are just getting started in their careers when, "Boom!", the conventional retirement age of sixty-five looms in the very near future. They are often not ready to retire. Their work is not yet done. They need more time to earn money. They need more time to reach their professional goals. They are healthy and energetic, and they are not psychologically prepared to retire. But there is a serious disparity between women's work lives and the policies and rules in many of the institutions of our society. Listening to our interviewees made that clear.

Each of the women in our cohort of interviewees is currently or has previously addressed the complex issue of work cessation that we call retirement. It is interesting to note that 32 percent of these women, age fifty-nine to ninety-two, were fully retired and another 32 percent were still working full time—an equal number at both ends of the spectrum. Surprisingly, age and income level were evenly dispersed as well. Yes, almost a third of our interviewees were still working full time in their sixties, seventies, and eighties. "No retirement for me!" many of them said. The fields in which these older workers have continued to work are nonprofit organization management, university administration, government agency management, university teaching, self-employment as a business owner, teaching children and adolescents, real estate brokering, consulting, and lecturing.

In addition, 20 percent were working in flexible situations that allowed them to work according to their own schedules. Those women were mainly artists, writers, nurses, teachers, and counseling practitioners. These professions are flexible in terms of time but demand a high level of self-discipline and independence. These interviewees had been pursuing their self-generating entrepreneurial work lives for a long time. They anticipated continuing in these pursuits as long as they were able to do so.

Finally, 16 percent were working part time in various positions: university teaching, leading workshops, doing nails, teaching art, caring for elderly hospice patients, and consulting. In sum, a full 68 percent of our interviewees were still working, while only 32 percent were fully retired. Regardless of their current work status, all our interviewees were very interested in discussing the issue of retirement. Still, most of them preferred to continue working for as long as possible, and all of them were mindful of the salient issues of work: its value to society, personal value, and means of income production.

Continuation of benefits, especially access to health insurance, was a major concern. We would anticipate that in the next few years, as the surge of baby boomers hits conventional retirement age, institutional and organizational policies that prohibit part-time and flexible work with benefits will begin to be challenged. It is likely that rigid mandatory retirement ages will also be contested as highly skilled and experienced workers become harder to replace and elderly employees decide not to give up the many satisfactions and payoffs they derive from work.

The entire workforce is changing as older people reach the mandatory age limits for retirement and often are not ready to retire, in many cases because they don't want to lose their health benefits. Health benefits based on prior employment will continue to become less available for retirees, as well as for those who are still working. We will have to create new methods for benefits to be distributed among a variety of ages in the workforce.

We will need to develop ways to appropriately reward those whose experience either adds value to changing workplaces or those who retrain to meet more modern workforce needs. It is a time for new and innovative changes to once again sweep the workforce, much as they did during the 1930s and 1940s in response to the Great Depression and World War II, in order to meet the needs and value the contributions of both men and women as they reach the final third of life.

## The Third-Third Transition (TTT)

As a result of the research conducted for this book, we have come to define this changing period of time in women's work lives as the "Third-Third Transition," or TTT, rather than "the retirement years." Since the women's movement of the 1960s and 1970s, women have entered and reentered the workforce in unprecedented numbers, and work outside the home now plays a pivotal role in women's lives. When changes in the work arena due to retirement begin to be anticipated or actually occur, all workers, including women, begin to feel anxious and off balance. They may be confused and perplexed as old habits give way to new structures and altered self-images. There may be a sense of crisis and impending loss, especially when one's sense of self and identity is closely tied to one's work role, title, or status in the community. We are a society that reveres important titles and pays homage to the power of positions, so when those titles and that power disappear, there is a sense of loss. These feelings and circumstances

61

mark the beginning of a significant life cycle transition, one we felt was so significant it required its own name.

According to Jill Tarule, there are four steps in the process of transformative change or transition.[5] The first step in this cycle is called diffusion. At this initial stage, we begin to feel confused and we lose our sense of equilibrium. Even though things may have been going well, when a period of transition begins, we are often perplexed and may be unable to explain what is going on and why we feel uneasy. Things around us seem diffuse, and things that used to seem simple begin to feel complex. The beginning of a transition is unnerving.

The next stage in the cycle of transition is called dissonance. At this point, we have a sense that we are out of synch with our environment. Things that had been working well before may now cause discontent and disjointed feelings. We are at odds with our circumstances. During our dissonant stage, we become uncomfortable with situations that were previously comfortable. We may notice that we disagree with our boss more frequently or that we are not as eager as we had been to attend staff meetings. We may become impatient with our friends and colleagues. We find ourselves talking about being burned out. We are ready for something new, but we can't seem to identify what that might be.

The third step in the transition process moves us toward differentiation. At this point, we are beginning to define our problem and we are gathering the energy to begin to solve it. Now we are beginning to feel much better. We are less confused, and our anxieties seem to be decreasing. Although we have not yet completely modified or redefined our new situation, we are well on our way toward doing so.

And finally, we reach forward to the last step, which we call coherence. At this stage, we begin to understand what has been happening to us and we start to redefine our lives. Perhaps we decide to change jobs. Perhaps we make a decision to retire. Whatever the specific decisions are, we begin to integrate our new circumstances into our lives and daily habits. When we have completed this fourth step, this particular transition has been completed and we are ready to live out the next phase of our lives.

Tarule's model of transition can be very helpful to people facing significant changes in their lives. When one thinks about the enormous changes in our daily lives when retirement occurs, it is clear that a mental model that explains the process of transition can be a helpful tool in understanding what we are experiencing.

One woman who was experiencing the ebbs and flows of the Third-Third Transition said that she "needed challenging activity—paid or not." She called retirement ridiculous and went on to say, "What am I going to do with my life? That's my question. We're searching for meaningful activities and need a language to address this time of life. There's no one solution. Self-understanding is the key." Another long-term career woman had a different perspective: "When you lose your title, what then? I don't want phased retirement. You're either in or out!" Taking a different position, a long-term teacher and administrator said, "I'm wrestling with phased retirement versus full retirement. I can work as long as I want to. There's no mandatory retirement here." So transitions look different to different people at different times. It can be useful to have a mental model through which one can view the transition experience.

## Adjusting to the Third-Third Transition (TTT): Small-Group Discussions

Consider how useful Tarule's model of transformative change could be for assisting women in adjusting to the Third-Third Transition in their work lives. One way of applying the model would be through small-group discussions and one-to-one therapy or mentoring sessions. These can be excellent support systems for women during these transitional times as they look for a new sense of coherence and integration in their lives.

One of the coauthors of this book experienced how a small-group discussion format can effectively support women during their TTT. A few years ago, two members of a women's organization invited other members who were considering retirement to convene informally around box suppers at the women's center of a nearby university. The event was called "A Conversation about Retirement and Transitions." Emphasis was not to be on the financial aspects of retirement, but on the psychological and social meaning of changing how we work and on what we focus on in later life. It was anticipated that the group would meet six times. Ten women attended the first evening session, and after a few meetings, the group had stabilized to include six women. The reasons given for not continuing in the group ranged from having busy travel and work schedules to needing time to care for infirm elderly parents.

The entire first evening discussion consisted of each woman introducing herself with a description of where she was in the process of considering retirement. The group listened attentively as each person candidly described her work life and current position and tried to define the issues that she was now facing regarding retirement. Brief, spontaneous, informal responses were made by members of the group to each others' presentations. The focus of the evening was listening. Before the evening ended, the group had decided to read a book on the subject, *The Way of Transition*, by William Bridges, and meet again in about a month to discuss it.

When the group returned for the second session, they compared notes and discussed a number of concepts from the book. Other books were recommended. The language of the group soon revolved around transitions, retirement, and reinvention. The group began to call itself a learning circle. The participants agreed that there were no adequate role models from their mothers' generation for this time of their lives and that they would have to learn from each other.

Throughout the six evenings, they exchanged stories, expressed their fears, and applauded each other's decisions. Spontaneous expressions typical of the TTT abounded:

- "Oh, to be seventy again!"
- "I'm in a neutral zone."
- "Will I be missed?"
- "We are the emeritus group."

- "What don't you want to do?"
- "What do you do when your husband retires? Do you spend all day every day together?"
- "Women continue to rebirth new life."
- "Being a grammy is probably not a full-time occupation."
- "I don't know how to let go."

By the end of the series of conversations, one woman had completely retired, cold turkey, from a business she had created. Another was anticipating retiring from her own business and was setting up a succession plan. A nonprofit organization administrator shared her anxieties as she announced a future date for her retirement to her staff and board. A recently retired workshop leader and teacher expressed pleasure and relief as she described her growing leisure travel schedule and her shrinking work schedule. A university administrator told of how she had extended her weekends by two days and was now into her phased retirement. She was rebalancing her time use and getting accustomed to her new equilibrium. New models of the TTT were beginning to emerge, and we knew real women who were actually using these models. Recommended books now included *Composing a Life*, by Mary Catherine Bateson, the daughter of Margaret Mead, and *My Time: Making the Most of the Bonus Decades after Fifty*, by Abigail Trafford.

By the time the next season rolled around, there was little need to continue the group. We had set out to explore together the rocky shoals of another life cycle transition, and we had done that. In the process, we had made some new friends, learned to articulate our concerns, and supported each other at a time when we all had felt somewhat confused, out of synch, and off balance. By the end of six small supper discussions that covered six months, we had all moved a stage or two in the transition cycle and were ready for the next step. Most of us had come through the first step, diffusion, and the second step, dissonance, and we had reached the third step, differentiation. We were creating new definitions and beginning to solve our so-called retirement problems as we each edged a bit closer to the stage of coherence and a new sense of harmony with our environments. The TTT had begun and was being negotiated by all of us. Once again, as women we had shared our issues with each other forthrightly and found friendship and support in each other. This small-group process, once called "consciousness raising," had worked as successfully as it had so many times before during the women's movement of the 1960s and 1970s. This informal small-group format had, once again, proven to be an effective problem-solving strategy for women.

The most consistent message from both our interviewees and the small-group discussions regarding the issues of work is that there is a real need for new work arrangements and retirement models for women in their third-third transitional years as they try to find a new equilibrium for making meaning in their lives when their work lives begin to shift and shrink.

It remains to be seen just how the work, retirement, and Third-Third Transition issues worked out by the current over-sixty women will be viewed by the 78 million baby boomers who follow them. It is often said that each generation must make its own decisions based on its own particular experiences and historical period. Offsetting this view is George Santana's famous quote that warns us, "Those who cannot learn from history are doomed to repeat it." We prefer to believe that learning can be transmitted intergenerationally and that women have learned that history does indeed matter.

## Baby Boomers Turn Sixty

One subject that is interesting when comparing the over-sixty Depression-era population with the post–World War II baby-boomer population is that of work values. Various studies of the workplace describe the value contrasts between these two segments of the population, as follows:

- **Business** – The Depression-era population favored big business and centralization, while the baby boomers are anti big business and favor decentralization.

- **Politics** – The Depression-era population is predominantly conservative, while the baby boomers are activists.
- **Technology** – The Depression-era population uses technology only as needed, and the baby boomers use technology voraciously.
- **Vision** – The Depression-era population is made up of long-term thinkers who are structured and absolute realists, while the baby boomers are short-term thinkers, spiritualists, and nonconformists.
- **Environment** – The Depression-era population views resources as commodities to be used, while the baby boomers view resources as commodities to be protected.
- **Personal Ethics** – The Depression-era population denies personal goals as motives for work, while the baby boomers see personal gratification as a key component of work.
- **Social** – The Depression-era population is essentially frugal, while the baby-boomer group is seen as materialistic.

These descriptors are a compilation of studies done in the late 1990s that were used by many corporations for strategic planning purposes.[6] They do not, however, differentiate between the genders, and appear to reflect mainly male value structures. From general observation as well as from our interviews, it would appear that Depression-era women, such as our interviewees, more closely resemble the reported baby-boomer values and therefore would be more in synch with today's population just turning sixty than with the males in their own age group. For example, when our interviewees described their work, very few had been employed by large corporations. Most were entrepreneurial in their work styles and had worked in nonhierarchical, decentralized environments that resembled those valued by the baby boomers more than those valued by the mostly male workers from the Depression era. Our female interviewees also reported that their personal goals were very important when selecting their work. This is similar to what the baby boomers say and in contrast to the selfless choices of sometimes dull work that most men of the Depression era made. The values of our over-sixty interviewees reflect flexible, creative, and innovative approaches to work. These women also argue for continuing to work for as long as possible and for transitions to part-time options in the workplace even when they are long past the traditional retirement age of sixty-five; the baby boomers are also interested in later life flexible work opportunities.

## A Recent Study of Baby Boomers

Demonstrating the work-related characteristics of the baby-boomer cohort is a recent study of baby boomers.[7] The study focused on the pre-retirement population, ages fifty-five to sixty-four, and investigated what this group of men and women envisioned for themselves over the next ten years, when they would be ages sixty-five to seventy-four, the same ages of many of the women we interviewed for this book. The results of the study showed that:

- Thirty-seven percent expect to be retired.
- Twenty-five percent expect to be working part time.
- Twenty percent expect to be fully engaged in a job or career.
- Twelve percent expect to be self-employed.
- Three percent expect never to be in the labor force.
- Two percent expect to be between jobs.

In other words, the majority (59 percent) of the baby-boomer respondents expected to be working after age sixty-five—full time, part time, running their own businesses, or being between jobs—and only 37 percent expected to be fully retired. These male and female baby boomers' expectations match the real experiences of our own female interviewees for this book, 68 percent of whom were still working and 32 percent of whom were retired, and thus are not a brand-new phenomenon. Therefore, those male and female boomers who are interested can find role models for their lives after sixty among the third-third women in the Depression-era generation that precedes them. Relative to both work and nonwork expectations, that same study of baby boomers also showed that:

- Ninety percent of the fifty-five- to sixty-four-year-old baby-boomer group is already spending more time with family and friends.
- Seventy percent would like to take classes for fun.
- Seventy percent would like to travel for fun.
- Sixty-eight percent would like to travel for work/service/learning.
- Fifty-seven percent already volunteer and 72 percent would like to volunteer in the future.
- Fifty-one percent would like to change to part-time or flexible work.
- Thirty-nine percent would like to have a leadership role in nonprofits.
- Only 37 percent would like to retire and not work.
- An additional 23 percent would like to start their own business.

In other words, the baby boomers expect to be able to combine work with other activities in mix-and-match ways, just as they have been doing throughout their adult lives. They are multitaskers. They choose flexible schedules. They love both their work and their play, and they combine family activities with other aspects of their lives. They are living full lives and expect to continue to do so. And many of them will choose to lead active lives that include work for as long as possible. These aspirations of the surveyed male and female baby boomers match those of the over-sixty female interviewees in our study. This finding shows again the potential role-model relationship between these two age groups.

In addition, this study reveals that the desire to travel for fun, to work, to do community service, and to continue to learn transcends ethnicity. The vast majority, 59 percent to 82 percent of whites,

Hispanics, and African Americans between the ages of fifty-five and sixty-four aspired to travel in the future. And from 52 percent to 70 percent of all ethnic groups from age fifty-five to sixty-four looked forward to taking classes for fun. More than 52 percent of whites and African Americans planned to work part time, while 53 percent of whites hoped to hold leadership positions in nonprofit agencies. An equal number of whites planned to volunteer. Denver, Colorado, was the location of this study, and Denver is considered to be the "Baby-Boomer Capital," with the highest percentage of boomers of any major US city. Thirty other markets were polled, but we do not have the results from those other cities.[8]

Some of our interviewees were in the group of early baby boomers just turning sixty. Their comments match the study quite well. One stated, "I want to mix and match part-time work and volunteering. There's no retirement for me!" Another referred somewhat obliquely to her limited finances and was decidedly practical: "I was a late bloomer. I'd like to retire, but I want to have the same lifestyle." A social worker who had just turned sixty was especially aware of the need to continue working, but was very positive about it: "Now that people are living longer and healthier, the definition of retirement is changing. I love working now. The years after sixty are a gift!"

## Institutional Change

Despite peoples' desires, however, be they baby boomers or older, many organizations and institutions are arranged to expect sixty-five-year-olds to retire. Part-time employment is not always feasible, because less-than-full-time employees may not be eligible for benefits such as health insurance. In addition, Medicare begins at age sixty-five and institutionalized benefit systems may not be able or willing to adjust their employee health insurance policies to make Medicare supplements available to active full- and part-time employees. In addition, some employers are getting rid of retirement benefits. So many employees may decide to retire just to preserve their health insurance and their pensions, even though they would prefer to continue to work.

Social Security may now begin at age sixty-two or sixty-five, although eligibility age is gradually increasing for those born in 1938 or after, until it reaches sixty-seven for those born after 1957. Once an employee elects to receive Social Security payments, her earning capacity may be limited by law. Some of us were able to collect both Social Security and an unlimited amount of earnings from a job, while others had to limit their earnings once they started to collect Social Security. Since these federal government rules have changed over the years and it is anticipated that they will change again soon, it is especially difficult for women to plan financially for their retirement years. Also, since many women have been in and out of the workforce over many years and their salaries are not yet equal to those of men ($.77 to the $1.00), over a lifetime women are likely to earn less than men who have the same educational credentials and even the same job titles. The result is that women often wish to continue to earn income for as long as possible. Social Security benefits can be delayed for just so long, then at seventy and a half one must begin to collect those benefits. If a person is not on Social Security but is a federal or state employee with a different retirement program, the rules and benefits may be entirely different.

Most work still occurs in organizations and institutions, be they for-profit businesses or nonprofit universities, government departments, community organizations, or agencies. In these organizations, there are elaborate rules and policies that are sometimes incompatible with individual circumstances. Fortunate is the woman or man who is an independent entrepreneur, investor, professional artist, or writer. These kinds of workers have the freedom to work whenever, wherever, and for as long as they want and are able.

## Unresolved Issues and Serious Consequences

The issues related to women's work were not only at the center of the women's movement of the 1960s and 1970s, they have persisted throughout the 1980s and 1990s and on into the twenty-first century. One unresolved issue that caught our attention was captured in a sign seen at a major thoroughfare years ago. It read "People who start late never catch up." While we can acknowledge that there are an infinite number of sequences of the various roles in women's lives, it is also clear that when one "stops out" or delays reentry into the workforce to have babies and rear children, one may lose workforce seniority and the concrete benefits that often go with it: promotions, salary increases, cumulative benefits, increased levels of retirement pay, Social Security formula growth, savings, and, ultimately, the capacity to generate income and to make investments. The result is that by starting later on their careers, women may never catch up and will pay a price for those delays in their later retirement years.

Another unresolved issue is hiring policies that favor younger workers. Many recruiters either overtly or subtly communicate that the older worker "need not apply." As women pass their own half-century mark at age fifty, they often express concern that they could not be hired if they lost their current job. Age discrimination is rampant, although difficult to prove. These kinds of practices and prejudices are foolish because older workers often have many traits and experiences that can benefit companies and institutions: loyalty, dependability, maturity, communication skills, leadership capacity, and various technical skills. As personnel shortages increase in coming years, it is predicted that employers will once again value older workers and seek them out.

We look forward to the day when institutions, government agencies, and businesses revise their workplace policies and practices to better match the needs of workers, especially female workers. By doing so, the quality of life for individual women and the quality of the workplace will increase. We are pleased that employers are beginning to realize the value of older workers. However we still have a long way to go before there is equality in the American workplace, especially for our older female population.

## Our Interviewees as Volunteers

Throughout the years, volunteering has played an important role in women's lives. In the late nineteenth and early twentieth centuries, women of financial means joined hands with immigrant women to establish many of the social-service agencies and child welfare institutions that still exist today.[9] Throughout the Depression years, women worked in soup kitchens to feed the hungry. During World War II, mothers rolled bandages for the Red Cross, collected "Bundles for Britain," served doughnuts at USO centers, and were plane watchers on roofs, looking out for enemy aircrafts. In the postwar years, women and girls became candy stripers and gift shop operators in hospitals, and during the civil rights, peace, women's, and environmental movements, women supplied most of the people power as volunteers in offices, protest marches, and campaigns. Churches and synagogues have always relied on women volunteers to supplement the work of the clergy. Political campaigns could not run without the help of volunteer women. In short, women do much of their work as volunteers, and millions of nonprofit agencies could not function without them. When Alexis de Tocqueville wrote *Democracy in America*, in 1848, he marveled at the volunteer spirit of our country, to which he attributed a good deal of our success as a democracy.

The interviewees in our study, who grew up before, during, and just after World War II, made history as the Greatest Generation. The eldest, now in their eighties and nineties, either volunteered themselves to serve in the women's auxiliaries of the armed forces or had boyfriends or husbands in the service. Said one eighty-seven-year-old interviewee, "During the war, I enlisted in the WAVES [Women Accepted for Voluntary Emergency Service, of the US Navy]. I loved it. We girls still meet."

Everyone pitched in during the war years. Everyone was a volunteer. The American volunteer culture has continued to this day and has provided a model for many other countries. There is even a new term to describe an entire global nonprofit sector: NGO, which stands for Non-Governmental Organization. Our ambassadors abroad frequently use the American model of nonprofits and volunteerism to strengthen citizen involvement in solving problems faced by other countries.

During and after the women's movement of the 1960s and 1970s, many of our charitable organizations complained that as women returned to the workplace, their agency volunteer ranks thinned. Then President John F. Kennedy challenged Americans to "ask not what your country can do for you, but ask what you can do for your country." Americans responded by the millions, joining the Peace Corps, Teacher Corps, SCORE, VISTA, and other federal government efforts to capitalize on our nation's altruism, intelligence, and skills to help other nations as well as our own inner cities. During the 1980s and 1990s, some effort was made to harness the increasing free time of retirees on behalf of civic improvements. During those decades, we saw the establishment of Foster Grandparents, Hope for the Children, the Experience Corps, the National Senior Service Corps, the Executive Service Corps, and other organizations that invited seniors to perform a variety of tasks on a volunteer basis, or with minimal compensation.[10] Today, retired physicians, nurses, and dentists board ships to provide health care to people around the world, retired attorneys do pro bono work for low-income clients, former public officials raise funds for emergencies on a global scale, and retired entertainers establish foundations and medical facilities that offer care on a sliding scale or for free.

## The Role of Volunteerism in Our Interviewees' Lives

Knowing the history of uncompensated volunteer work in women's lives, we asked our interviewees, "Are you volunteering now? Where? Compare your current volunteering to past years." The responses revealed both expected and unexpected comments. Most of the women had volunteered throughout their lives, even when they were working and raising families. They volunteered for the PTAs of their children's schools, the Girl Scouts and Boy Scouts, their churches and synagogues, various community organizations with causes they believed in, the League of Women Voters, political campaigns, and every type of nonprofit imaginable. They had served on the boards of directors of nonprofit organizations and pursued social justice goals.

Currently, 36 percent were serving on boards, some on more than one. Some thought such service had been overrated; others were tired of being asked to contribute and then being involved in endless discussions at board meetings where their opinions were tolerated, but not valued. These negative responses reflect a weariness with volunteer work that might be unexpected. But having had a lifetime of volunteer experiences ourselves, we understood these responses. Just how many more fund-raising dinners does one want to go to? How many more PTA meetings, homeowners' debates? How much more precinct walking? The needs in the community are endless and unrelenting. For some, it was time to retire from the volunteer sector and find a new way to contribute to society, where it was considered more useful or provided for their own continued growth.

An equal number of our interviewees said that they were not doing any volunteer service at present due to time constraints or loss of interest. Another 24 percent said that they respond to requests for their services when asked, and 20 percent talked about donating money to various causes. A few who were especially fortunate had established family foundations and distributed sizable amounts of money annually. These foundations had become management projects and often required considerable time for administration and the prudent management of investment of the family's funds. A few interviewees who had not yet retired indicated that they planned to spend at least some of their free time after retirement volunteering in their ethnic or religious communities. They understood the value of their roles as mentors to younger women and looked forward to giving back after having had successful careers themselves.

"I've served on volunteer boards all my life," said one eighty-seven-year-old interviewee. "I retired at eighty-four, but I still volunteer," said another active woman. Another interviewee, who had been very active in her community and was now in poor health asked, "Women are not being properly utilized at this time of life. We have to redefine ourselves." Even with her disability, this mid-seventies woman was volunteering her time to work on a historical-museum project in her town. Transitions are never easy, but having a positive attitude and forward-looking self-image helps.

After observing and participating ourselves in many agencies and organizations that utilize volunteers, we believe that a great deal will need to be done to attract and retain the volunteer energies of current and future retirees. This will require a one-to-one counseling effort on a grand scale in order to meet the needs of both the agencies and the volunteers. There is huge potential for increased volunteerism in the up-and-coming baby-boomer group who have been primarily focusing on their families and careers during the second third of their lives. We anticipate that central offices and regional networks will begin to be formed that have the capacity to handle the recruitment, training, coordination, and evaluation of volunteers for multiple organizations and agencies. Like the referral and information services of the sixties and seventies, these networks, if thoughtfully and carefully designed and implemented, have the potential to enrich and sustain our needy nonprofit sector. At the same time, the appropriate evaluation and coordination of volunteers with activities that interest them and in which they have some skills and talents could support and improve the quality of life for many retirees who, without such guidance, might be bored, lonely, and depressed. In such cases, health begins to deteriorate and the quality of life itself decreases. And the retirees would then be lost to the volunteer sector entirely and would remain underutilized by our society, which is in dire need of support in many sectors of civic life.

At this time in our country's history, we need new and innovative ways to unify our increasingly diverse population. As our aging population grows, we also need new and innovative methods that can capture the energies of our healthy, highly skilled, patriotic, and civically responsible citizens. Volunteer activities, in service to our common goals and humanity, can strengthen our country, our communities, and our people. We hope that our up-and-coming leaders take these possibilities seriously and begin to create the infrastructures that can be effective in mobilizing these kinds of initiatives.

## Family, Work, and Volunteerism

If one were to draw a pie chart that represented the activities of a contemporary American woman's life, that circle would likely be divided into various-sized slices representing family, work, and volunteerism. Each of our charts would be a visual representation of how we have deployed our energies at various stages of our lives. The sizes of the slices of the pie would reflect the infinite sequences and shifting priorities of our lives at different times in our lives. There might be years when the family slice was close to 100 percent of the pie, and other years when work, volunteerism, and family each were represented by a third of the pie, in a more balanced-life allocation. Times of transition are really attempts to reallocate the size of the slices of pie so that they match our changing needs and realities.

The pie chart that represents our Third Third Transition varies for each of us. It may be helpful to actually trace out this chart as a kind of an exercise during periods of reinvention, redefinition, and transition in order to get a handle on how your slices are labeled and how big to make them. Based on our interviews, it would seem that most women over sixty will be shrinking the work slice while increasing the family slice. The volunteer slice is the most variable, ranging from being entirely invisible to occupying more than half of the pie. But however the pies is sliced, in many respects, women's work is still never done.

# CHAPTER 5

# Women and Money

**The greatest of evils and the worst
of crimes is poverty.**
—George Bernard Shaw, *Major Barbara*

## Gender Differences Regarding Money

When working women get together, they usually do not talk about money. In contrast, when men get together, they usually talk about those aspects of life designed to acquire money: their jobs, investments, the stock market, real estate, future employment, retirement, and the like. Men find these conversations compelling, and often they get hints, tips, or leads about possible investments and new ways to make money. Women are not often privy to these kinds of conversations and have relatively few informal sources of information about how to make money.

Men also talk about sports. Sports are competitive, and sports provide men with a large arena where they learn, from an early age, how to be fair, highly competitive, and winners or losers. As a rule, women now in their sixties or older did not usually participate in sports at this level, or if they did, they were probably thought of as being "different" by their peers. There were few opportunities for most women to participate in competitive sports before the passage of Title IX of the Education Amendments of 1972 to the US Civil Rights Act of 1964. Title IX prohibits sex discrimination against students and employees of educational institutions. Before these pieces of federal legislation, only a small percentage of girls, mostly those who attended girls' summer camps, girls' schools, and women's colleges, had significant experience with competitive sports. Those who attended coeducational public schools and colleges had minimal and, at best, uneven experiences with competitive sports. The relationship between learning the rules of sports and the rules of money has just begun to be understood.

When men talk about money as adults, it is easy to see that they might also be talking about sports. They apply the same rules and winning habits that they learned in competitive sports to the game of making money. In these conversations, men learn about money: how to get it, how to make it, how to keep it, how not to lose it, and how to grow it. This shared information about money sometimes also has a competitive edge, as is true in competitive sports. Everyone wants to be a winner, just like they were on the ball field. Shared information increases both the ability to "win" and the sense of competition. Men have learned how to manage this conflict and benefit from it. Men understand this kind of talk. For the most part, women have not had this kind of experience. As a result, they don't engage in this subject when they talk together.

This is changing among younger women, especially for those who have had experience with sports or who have gone to business school. But the fact remains that most women who are now age sixty or older are at a severe disadvantage when it comes to talking about money. They typically didn't study finance in school. Their parents rarely tutored them about money. They usually didn't discuss it among themselves, either as younger or older women. They rarely read books about it. And, if they are married, they frequently rely on their husbands to manage the family's investments and financial decisions. Even though today, the woman in the family may more regularly spend most of the money or have a say in how it is spent, that was not older women's reality when they were young. Even with the changes in the present atmosphere regarding women and money, when it comes to large purchasing decisions—a home, a car, a vacation, a home renovation—in the majority of households, it is often still the man who takes the lead and ultimately makes those financial decisions, even after some conferencing with his wife.

Among women in their third thirds, however, there are some exceptions, examples of women who were and are quite savvy with money. For example, (1) women who remained or became single, and

(2) women who earned more money than their mates and thereby may have gained more control over their own earnings. Those women have often become quite adept at earning, saving, and investing.

But for the majority of women in the third third of their lives, learning about finances, budgeting, saving, and investing has been difficult. Further, much of what they are now becoming aware of they may not fully understand and use. Those who can afford it often hire a financial advisor. Some join an investment group and learn about the stock market and real estate with other women. Others just muddle along.

## Money and Control

The management of money is one of the primary methods of one person gaining or maintaining control over another. Whoever controls the money controls the patterns of daily life within a household. The psychological advantage in the relationship is thus held by the money manager. Additionally, if one of the adults in the family does not have control over expenses or investments or, at minimum, input into them, they are left with a dearth of information that might become vitally important to them in the future. If one does not control one's own earnings, which are some of the fruits of employment, then retirement decisions cannot be made wisely. The same is true of decisions about purchasing a home, the distribution of earnings in the family, financial decisions about children's education, and decisions about where to live in retirement. It is very difficult to be faced with major financial concerns when the person who previously made all the financial decisions has died or left the household. The less control over money and money management a woman has, the less experience and competence she will have with which to make important decisions about her own future.

For many women now in the third phase of their lives, this lack of control and knowledge regarding money has created a real problem in terms of their financial welfare, and this situation materially affects their entire life and well-being. Many of these women have had to learn quickly how to become the major financial manager of the household, often in emotionally stressful times when their spouse is ill or dying or when a divorce is under way.

## Money and Marital Discord

In most contemporary families, the husband and the wife now share responsibility for the acquisition and management of money. Still, marriage counselors and divorce attorneys tell us that the issue of money is the most significant issue in marital discord, even more so than sex. Couples argue about money and who controls it more than they argue about their children. In many families, all earnings still go into a joint account, and any effort by a woman to have her own checking or savings account is often met with resistance and perhaps downright hostility. So stashing money in the proverbial cookie jar seems to be alive and well even in many modern homes: women still save money out of their household allowances. And while some women are able to keep their inheritances from their mothers, fathers, or other relatives in separate bank accounts or investments, many husbands still believe that they have equally inherited those assets. In fact in some states, husbands may have a legal right to sharing in the inheritance.

Disagreements over these kinds of sensitive matters may be viewed as disloyalty, lack of love, disrespect, lack of trust, or lack of confidence. Issues of dominance and control often underlie many of these financial debates. Because women traditionally have had less depth of knowledge of financial affairs, they are often at a disadvantage during these discussions. Fortunately, women are becoming more money wise.

## Money and the Women's Movement

During the women's movement of the 1960s and 1970s, many of the topics that were at issue revolved around money and its distribution. Some examples are equal pay for equal work; lack of access to high level executive positions; patterns of women working in low paying human service jobs such as teaching, social work, and nursing; few women on corporate boards; women not being able to get credit in their own names; male cosignatures required for major purchases and loans for large items such as cars and homes; alimony and child support payments in a divorce being kept to a minimum or withheld entirely; and dozens of other issues that were couched in neutral language but were essentially financial discrimination issues.

Our society is not very far from the days when the concept of "woman as chattel" was embedded in our laws, policies, procedures, and customs. And it is easy to find examples even today of beliefs in the inferiority of women in other societies: burkas as required dress in some parts of the Middle East, denial of education to girls by the Taliban in Afghanistan, absence of a woman's right to own property in many sub-Saharan African countries, female genital mutilation, and the practice of aborting female fetuses in China. All of these issues are connected to women's status relative to money, societal issues, and male dominance and control.

As women have gained freedom to be treated as individuals of worth, they have asserted their presence in issues dealing with their financial rights. Concurrently, their financial know-how has increased. They have learned to think, plan, and act according to financial constraints. As women have gained some measure of financial independence, they have also gained comparable worth and freedom in other areas of their societies. An excellent example is the growth of female small-business micro-loans that foster the success of new entrepreneurs and productive small-manufacturing businesses in parts of Africa and the Far East. Liberty and the control of one's own money go hand in hand.

## Money and Health: Basics for Positive Aging

It was clear that our interviewees and discussion group participants believed that two things were primary in fostering a successful old age: money and health. In calculating their "retirement equation," some women found that these two primary variables were inextricable. They talked freely and expressed concerns such as, "If I keep my health, I will be okay financially" or "I have enough to live well if I am well." Most were concerned about remaining independent and not becoming a burden, financially or otherwise, to their families if they were to become so ill they could not live alone. A realistic, witty remark came from more than one of them that, paraphrased together, might be, "If my legs, brain, bank account, and love of living stay in balance, I'll make it through whatever the health care expenses are for at least the next twenty or thirty years…If not, I'll have to go back to work."

As they considered what they would advise younger women about money, the same sentiment was expressed by many of our interviewees, "Learn everything you can about your own affairs, be involved with money decisions in your household and your life, save as much as you can, and plan ahead…always ahead!"

## Women and Money in Today's World

In 2004, the most recent data we have, the average life expectancy of an American woman was 80.4 years and the average life expectancy of an American man was 75.2 years.[1] On average, women are expected to live 5.2 years longer than men. Add to that difference the fact that most women marry men who are older than themselves, and it is reasonable to expect that most married women will live alone as widows for at least five to ten years in their older years. In addition, there are an increasing number of single women who do not marry or who get divorced. "The proportion of never-married women rose to nearly a quarter of the electorate between 1972 and 2006, up from 15%. Overall, never-married, divorced or widowed women are now a narrow majority of adult women, and unmarried households are now a majority of the nation's households."[2]

It is clear that there is an increasing number of women living alone during the third third of their lives. Most women over sixty, regardless of their original marital status, will be required to access, manage, invest, and conserve financial resources for five to twenty years—and for some of the growing number of female centenarians, for as many as twenty-five years. Although these projections are always imprecise, common sense tells us that it is critical that women become more competent in the area of finance than they may now be.

## Mother's Day Data

The weeks around Mother's Day are favorite times for researchers and government agencies to release studies on changes in women's lives. In May 2007, *The Denver Post* and *Rocky Mountain News* reported, based on a national survey, that the value of a stay-at-home mom's work was estimated to be $138,095 a year, up 3 percent from 2006.[3] That assumes a ninety-two-hour work week, with forty hours of regular pay and fifty-two hours of overtime. So, if the value of women's work were included in her Social Security accumulations, the payment levels at retirement would rise considerably. Additionally, if a husband lost his wife to death or divorce and needed to hire housekeeping and child-rearing help, that would be a very large expense.

Also in 2007, reports showed that unequal levels of pay still exist: "77 cents is what women earn for every dollar men earn. For black women, that drops to 72 cents. For Hispanic women, the rate is 59 cents for every dollar."[4] These are overall figures and women's earnings vary by field. Women earn the following percentages of what men earn in selected fields: engineer: 82 percent; computer programmer: 81 percent; professor: 77 percent; accountant: 75 percent; and lawyer: 70 percent.[5]

In addition, salary gaps between the sexes grow over time: "A gap in pay between US college-educated men and women starts soon after graduation and widens over time...One year after receiving degrees, women working full time already earned 20 percent less than men...The difference grew to about 30 percent a decade after graduation...Even after controlling for hours, occupation, parenthood and other factors, the [AAUW] study found that one quarter of the pay gap remains unexplained. The group said that portion of the gap is 'likely due to sex discrimination.'"[6] It is estimated that the "amount, over a lifetime, a working woman and her family lose because of the wage gap totals $700,000 to $2,000,000."[7] Other studies and government data corroborate these findings.

Although many people think that issues regarding women and wages have been addressed and there is equality of pay in the labor market, this is not so. What this means for women over sixty who are approaching retirement is threefold: (1) having earned less than men, women are likely to have saved less than men; (2) having earned less than men, women are likely to have accumulated less in their Social Security accounts and, therefore, will collect less when they begin their Social Security payments; and (3) having earned less than men, women are likely to have invested less and will have a smaller nest egg when they cease working.

On the other hand, working women are not only made up of independent single breadwinners: they are often married. A study of the 67 million married US working women shows "a growing equity among couples when it comes to income, decision-making, parenting and housekeeping."[8] Working wives appear to provide stability at home, according to Penn State University sociologist Stacy Rodgers and her colleagues.[9] Their research shows that women's contributions to family incomes rose from 21 percent in 1980 to 32 percent in 2000. At the same time, divorce rates have declined to their lowest rates since 1970 and now stand at 3.6 per 1,000 people in the United States, down from 5.3 divorces per 1,000 people in 1981.[10] An important conclusion drawn from these studies is that "families with two earners with good jobs have seen an improvement in their standard of living, which leads to less tension at home and lower probability of divorce."[11] It is clear from these numbers that as women have increasingly become part of the labor force, divorce has decreased and equity within marriage has increased. If a reduction in the wage gap and more equitable wages for women were added to these positive trends, it would seem that not only women would benefit, but also their marriages, their spouses, their families, and their future retirement. There is little to lose and everything to gain from reducing the wage gap and increasing salary equity among workers. However, while this will aid the next generation of working women, the cultural and financial lag still exists for the current population of women above age sixty. They still feel significant financial pressures as they try to plan for the days when they will no longer be working. Women on pensions or other retirement plans may have had little input into those plans. Therefore, today's older women may need more support now than women in the future may need. This is especially true of those who are at a lower economic level than our interviewees. It is important that we do not leave these women alone and in financial distress while we, who are better off, tackle our own future issues.

## Financial Status of Our Interviewees

Even though we did not plan to interview a socioeconomically and statistically balanced sample of women in a wide variety of financial circumstances for this book, we did want to be able to present a realistic picture of the differing financial circumstances of our interviewees. Among them, from a financial perspective, 81 percent felt financially comfortable, 14 percent felt secure or very well-off, and 14 percent could be described as having modest financial resources. The majority were middle class or upper middle class in terms of their present wealth. That's more of a normal bell curve than we anticipated for a nonstratified sample. While this group of women may have been a bit wealthier than the average of all American women above sixty, they were fairly representative of women who had worked during the second third of their lives.

While this book focuses mainly on middle-class women, we must continue to be interested in and concerned about those women who met many obstacles in their working life: lack of educational opportunities, inability to get and hold a job with good wages and benefits, divorce or death of spouse with the consequent severe alteration of lifestyle, or confinement to low-paying jobs for whatever reason. As these working-class women age, many of them are prevented from making attractive housing decisions and sustaining themselves adequately. We respect their efforts to support themselves, while at the same time remain attentive to ways that our society must find ways to support their needs.

## In Sickness and in Health: A Financial Variable

Even as traditional marriage vows anticipate life's ups and downs, few of us are prepared psychologically or financially for the need to care for a chronically ill spouse or family member. The marital status of our interviewees was as follows: 65 percent were married at the time of the interview, 18 percent were widowed, 13 percent were divorced, and 5 percent were single. This mix of circumstances among our interviewees relative to a spouse is typical of the total US population of women in the third third of their lives: about two-thirds of them are married.

But our interviewees' responses about money in light of their marital situations and health provided some interesting patterns. About half of the interviewees had husbands or other close relatives who required a high level of care for chronic health conditions: diabetes, heart disease, cancer, stroke, Parkinson's disease, blindness or severely restricted vision, and Alzheimer's disease or other memory loss condition. These health conditions were both costly and confining for the wives as well as the husbands. When the chronically ill person was the husband, the couple's health insurance rates and out-of-pocket medical expenses had increased, sometimes home renovations and alterations were required to accommodate disabilities, at times short-term in-home professional care was needed, as were special meals and diets, and periodic hospital costs and rehabilitation and nursing home expenses had an impact on the family's financial situation. When the health conditions belonged to other relatives, complete or partial dependency resulted and was often both financially draining and psychologically stressful. Clearly these are expensive requirements that negatively impact even comfortable middle-class budgets.

Almost half of the married women had to both care for their husbands personally and provide costly professional care for them. About half of these caretaker women were still working, and the other half had retired. All of them would have preferred to continue to work, but some had been forced to alter their personal retirement plans to devote their full time to their husbands. In the process, their level of financial security had changed and their financial futures were a cause for concern. These situations reveal that health is actually a financial variable; the two issues are inextricably entwined.

## For Richer and For Poorer

About a third of our interviewees had husbands who were healthy and did not require their wives' daily care. All of them, except one who herself was in ill health, were still working at least part time and were focused on how they wanted to rebalance and redefine their retirement years. In financial terms, they would all be described as comfortable, but were concerned about the potential expense of catastrophic illness for either themselves or their husbands should one of them fall ill. They were, for the most part, healthy and highly functional. They were talented and well-educated professional women. They had healthy and supportive spouses. They were living in the same homes that they have lived in for many years or were downsizing to smaller homes that relieved them of the day-to-day responsibilities of home maintenance. Their financial circumstances were decidedly middle class. Now they could afford most of what they might want or need. They had discretionary income. They traveled and went out to dinner and shows. They were active in their communities. They continued to grow and be productive. They were not necessarily interested in retiring, and many of them preferred to keep working for as long as they could.

This is the group that the advertisers are hoping will consider retirement community living, that travel agents are trying to interest in going on a Caribbean cruise or to Europe. This is the group that stockbrokers and financial advisors invite to free meals at fine restaurants in hopes of gaining a new account. This group takes courses, reads books, and goes to concerts and lectures. This group continues to enhance the economy today. And this very fortunate group is the "positive aging" model to which working, middle-class, baby-boomer women are looking to in their quest for well-being and the good life after sixty.

## 'Til Death Do Us Part

Most of the widows, who made up 18 percent of our interviewees, could be described as well-off. One was no longer working after she sold her successful business, and three had more-than-sufficient financial resources based on their late husbands' financial success. The remainder, who could be described as living modestly or being comfortable, were still working well into their seventies and eighties. These women not only needed their salaries, but expressed joy and pleasure in their work. Retirement was not their immediate goal.

One widow, who was still teaching school in her mid-seventies, said, "I'm trying to live on what I make. I'll work until I can't anymore. I need the health insurance that comes with my job." She indicated that there was no mandatory retirement age in her school district and then reported that she had experienced age discrimination in another school where she had been teaching previously. She continued, "My son looks after my investments, which are the funds I received from the sale of my previous home. We spent all our savings on my late husband's health care before he died. I'm fortunate that my kids can help me if I ever need them."

Another widow said that she had a financial advisor on whom she depended to continue the successful investment program that her late physician husband had started. She stated, "I have no financial worries." By contrast, a third, eighty-seven-year-old widow who has worked hard and lived modestly all her life, said, "Thank goodness for Social Security! I would worry if I didn't have Social Security." She had bought her own condo under the GI Bill, having served in the armed forces during World War II. She had car payments and was saving her earned income for trips and other extras.

It is clear that becoming widowed leaves women in greatly varied financial conditions.

## On Their Own

Most of the 13 percent of our interviewees who were divorced were still working into their sixties and seventies. They spoke about retirement, but had not yet wanted to give up either their income or their meaningful work. One divorced woman of modest means expressed a high level of anxiety about growing older and anticipating retirement. "I am worried about 'what ifs,'" she said. She was uncertain if her finances would permit her to retire, and she needed professional financial planning advice, which she did not yet have. "I don't know if I can afford a financial advisor. But I don't know much about money and have a lot of anxiety about retirement and investing without one," she mused. "I'm very worried if I'll have enough money if I retire," she continued. A handicapped dependent son who will never be self-sufficient compounds this woman's situation.

This interviewee is typical of many working women who have spent their early adult years caring for children and finishing school and subsequently find themselves at relatively low levels of Social Security income or retirement investments and savings. If divorce occurs, the pressure increases on these women to earn as much as possible, though their capacity to earn is relatively modest. In addition, these working women often have little financial background with which to make wise investment decisions and usually have limited knowledge of qualified professionals and resources that could assist them. On top of this, they may have no concept of how expensive financial planning services can turn out to be. This may be one of the most vulnerable groups in our society. While they have followed the rules and labored earnestly and long, they are easy potential victims of scams, get-rich-quick schemes, and have few people in their families or environments who are both competent and willing to guide them. They live modestly and have little extra cash at the end of each month. By and large, these women are hidden from our view and are not poor enough to be eligible for social services, while not being financially able to live a very comfortable lifestyle. They worry about money all the time and are a bit nervous about retiring, lest they have insufficient funds to live on. Although these women rely on senior centers and community groups for many services, as a society we should be shining a spotlight on their situation and assisting them through their later years.

A few other divorced women among our interviewees, who are at the opposite end of the spectrum and who had been married to substantially wealthy men, had received generous financial settlements at the time of their divorce and were not concerned about their own financial futures. They continued to work for their own pleasure and satisfaction but were not dependent on their incomes for sustenance or future security. One put it this way: "I'm lucky. I plan on dying with money in my pocket. I have enough money from my divorce settlement. Having a financial planner would be like going on a diet. But I worry about things I can't control." She went on to say, "Women don't talk to other women about money. Men always talk about money. Women should learn to make investments together, like men do."

Still other divorced interviewees had secured professional employment that had significant retirement benefits: pensions at large percentages of their salaries, 401Ks matched by their employer, investment opportunities, transition counseling, financial planning, and health insurance with premiums at least partially paid by the employer. In fact, these divorced women had consciously embarked on midlife career changes, with an eye toward retirement benefits. Those benefits were one of the mandatory requirements for accepting a job, even if starting salaries seemed low. As single women, they assumed that they would have to support themselves for the rest of their lives and knew that it was up to them to make sure they could live in the style to which they were accustomed once they retired. These were some of the most financially savvy of all of our interviewees over sixty.

## Shared Financial Circumstances

While the remaining 5 percent of our interviewees were single by choice, all of them were living in relationships with other women, some in one-to-one arrangements and others in group and community arrangements. Their financial situations were similar to the married women in that they were in interdependent relationships with others relative to money. They were less alone than the widows and less troubled than the divorcees. Financially, they were relatively knowledgeable and had been functioning independently relative to money for many years. One unmarried woman summed up her situation in this way: "I'm fortunate. I saved money while I was working for the state and have a good pension. My financial situation is almost the same as when I was working. I don't have a financial planner, and my investments are in mutual funds. I have health insurance. I'm not worried about money."

## Changing Economic Circumstances

The first financial question that we asked in our interviews was focused on the changing personal economic circumstances that the interviewees might have encountered after age sixty. Surprisingly, most (64 percent) of our interviewees said that they had few anxieties about money at this stage of their lives and that there were no immediate economic changes they needed to make. Among this relatively secure group were women who were married, widowed, single, and divorced. In many ways, they were living in a "new frontier" of life among women who were aging. They were happy women who had learned life's lessons and enjoyed their present stage of life.

The remaining women (36 percent) were less certain that their money was sufficient to last until they died or would support them comfortably for the rest of their lives. This less-secure group also was varied in terms of marital status: married, divorced, widowed, and single. However, all of them were the main breadwinners in their households. Money was one of the most important variables in their decision making. All of them expressed great concern about having enough money as well as knowing how to safeguard the principal while growing their interest through investments. Some of them were relying on external financial advisors to guide them; others were not. But they all expressed some level of anxiety about money and were not confident about their own knowledge and capacity to manage their funds properly and profitably. This was a financially vulnerable group of women who might gain both confidence and increased competence from learning more about money and how to invest it.

## Financial Planning and Strategies

We then inquired about what preplanning and financial strategies our interviewees had used to address their financial challenges at this stage of their lives. Most of them were simultaneously employing multiple financial strategies; therefore, the following percentages exceed 100 percent.

## Social Security

The two most common sources of financial support, not surprisingly, were Social Security payments and investments. Most of the interviewees were receiving funds from these two sources. Understandably, recent proposals to privatize Social Security had little or no support from this group. The financial foundation that Social Security provided was important to all of them, regardless of their level of income. One interviewee in her early seventies, who was quite comfortable and had multiple sources of income, including employment, had contributed all of her Social Security payments to charity. She was very proud and pleased that it was possible for her to do this. In contrast, another interviewee of very modest means stated that she relied heavily on her Social Security payments for daily support, although she was supplementing that income by working part time in a position that made her life more meaningful. She was eighty-seven and delightfully busy.

## Pensions and Annuities

Forty-five percent of the interviewees, or their spouses, were receiving or were eligible for a pension or an annuity. This income varied widely; for some it was a substantial portion of their highest earned salary and for others it was modest payments from mutual fund companies or other annuity sources. In most cases, prior employers had matched the employee's monthly contributions to these retirement funds, and in all cases these funds were greatly appreciated and key to sustaining a comfortable lifestyle.

However, the present economy bodes poorly for sustained employer contributions to retirement funds. A look at today's benefits plans shows a tendency toward reducing the employers' costs and increasing the employees' contributions. Also, the traditional "cradle-to-grave" employment patterns, where people work for only one employer over their lifetimes, are no longer available. And employees today have only short-term loyalty to their companies and do not usually plan to stay in one position or with one employer for their entire work life. Two exceptions to these changes in traditional lifelong employment patterns are government and academic employment, where employees often remain in their initial organizations throughout their careers. One reason for this is that the benefit packages are often very attractive and generous in the public sector compared to what is offered in the private sector.

Because most employer-based retirement packages are changing, well before age sixty women need to do new kinds of financial planning, both within their own employment settings and those of their partners, in order to ensure that their retirement plans will be able to support their lifestyles and provide them with income at a reasonable level after they stop working.

One interviewee in her nineties who had worked as a professional throughout her adult life now had a second husband who had Alzheimer's disease and was in a nursing home. "I'm the breadwinner now," she said in a matter-of-fact tone. "I'm in control of our money and investments. I feel sorry for women who never learned about money. The nursing home costs $70,000 per year, and he's been there for six years already," she confided. "We have insurance and retirement funds, in addition to Social Security," she continued. It was fortunate that she not only had enough sources of funds to support her husband's nursing home costs, but that she felt comfortable about making investments and being in control of their funds.

## Work

More than two-thirds of our sixty- to over-ninety-year-old interviewees were still working and receiving income from their work. Some were self-employed; others were employed by other companies and organizations. Whether the woman had already retired or was anticipating doing so, they all spoke of valuing their work not only for the income it generated, but also for the satisfactions it provided them.

While some expressed an eagerness to retire in order to have more free time to pursue other interests, others were quite concerned that without their paycheck and their work they would become unhappy and insecure. Many said that their identities and sense of self were tied to their work. Their status in the community was partially based on the titles of their present positions. Their major intellectual stimulation and challenges were derived from their work. They were anxious about how they would spend their time without having an office to go to. There were few women ahead of them providing retirement role models that showed them what life would be like when their paid employment ended.

Many of those who were married worried about having to be home all day with their husbands, especially if their spouses had different interests than they had. Those who were single, divorced, or widowed were still relying on their work situations for companionship and sociability. They dreaded the loneliness that retirement might bring. Work for many of these women had never been seen as instrumental, in other words, only a means to an end: income. Work was most often viewed by these women as an end in itself: a source of pride, stimulation, and satisfaction. Discussions during our interviews about work often lasted longer than other topics. For women now older than sixty, perhaps the force behind their individual drive to work and have success was to establish a singular recognition of their talents that was not common in prior generations of women. They saw their work as an individual expression of their ability and growth. In these new work roles, they have laid the groundwork for the women who follow them who also value their work and their unique contributions to the workplace.

One married, self-employed woman in her mid-sixties said that she loves her work and is now working only when she wants to. In discussing money, she explained, "I will run the economic engine. We've planned well. Things are set. Money is not worrisome to us." She went on to explain that she and her second husband lived modestly, traveled in the context of their work, and understood that it is a luxury that they don't have to worry about money.

## Financial Settlements and Inheritances

A few of our interviewees had received an inheritance or a financial settlement of some kind. These financial resources had come in the form of either lump sum payments or periodic annuity payments. Receiving these funds had often changed the way they viewed the third third of their lives. These sources of income were parents, sisters, other relatives, deceased husbands, and ex-husbands. In each instance, the acquired funds had either not been anticipated or were negotiated, but in either case, they had provided a significant level of financial security and were welcomed by the recipient, whose lifestyle and sense of security had been measurably improved by receiving them.

One eighty-four-year-old interviewee whose over-ninety-year-old husband had a chronic heart condition had received an annuity from her wealthier, now deceased sister. As a result, she receives funds monthly that supplement their Social Security and her husband's pension from a job in state government. When asked about money issues in her life, she said confidently, "As we've gotten older, it's become easier. We don't need to watch every penny. We're even able to help our kids. We live in our home, which we own and is paid for. We have help that comes in to clean and do some caregiving, as we need that. We are very fortunate." These changes in this family's financial circumstances during their older years were for the better, even though they had lived a fairly modest middle-class life. This woman said with a smile, "I have no anxieties about money." What a wonderful thing to be able to say!

## Savings versus Investments

Some of the interviewees referred to savings as a financial strategy. Perhaps they distinguished savings from investments by thinking of savings as cash in a bank and investments as stocks, bonds, and real estate. In any case, this comparatively small group indicates that the concept of savings has largely been replaced by the notion of investments, which might include money market accounts and certificates of deposit. A full 86 percent of our interviewees had investments: stocks, bonds, mutual funds, real estate, businesses, and other assets. Most of the women were actively engaged in managing their investments either with partners or alone. Some relied on a financial advisor for expert advice and had some measure of trust in their advice.

"Money is a motivator for me," said one married woman in her late sixties who was not typical among our interviewees. "We keep separate accounts. I want my own spending money," she continued, "and that's just fine with my husband. We each have our own stock investment accounts, and I make my own charitable contributions. We don't want to be a drain on our children, and we are helping them now, since we can." Both the husband and wife were working according to their own schedules. They enjoyed their work and had opportunities to continue to work for as long as they wished. They were more sophisticated about money than many of our interviewees. In contrast to those married couples who pooled their incomes, bank accounts, and investments and where the husband dominated the financial decision making, this marriage was more of a relationship among equals. They dealt with financial matters in collaborative and mature ways, just as they dealt with other aspects of their lives. The story of how they developed this type of egalitarian arrangement and how the woman became knowledgeable about handling money should be told to baby boomers who are looking for enlightened marital role models.

## Collaborative Finances

One of our interviewees, who relied on a women's religious community for her financial support, revealed an interesting model for the third third of life. All members of the community had worked throughout their lives and pooled their incomes. In addition, various donations were also pooled and applied to the community's common housing and health facilities. The members of the community had come from families with varying levels of wealth, yet once they joined the community, they shared equally in the total community's assets. "We learn how to conserve money," she said. "We are conscious of not overusing resources. I must do a budget and can't spread the funds too thin. We support many projects and make community decisions about which

98

projects to invest in." When it comes time to retire, all members of the community can choose to live at their motherhouse or remain in a retirement facility that they owned in another location. Housing, meals, clothing, and health care are provided for. And community life includes intellectual and volunteer pursuits.

We could all learn a great deal about managing money from this kind of women's community. Such long-term, religiously based communities can serve as a model for other unmarried women in the third third of their lives, be they single, divorced, or widowed.

## Financial Planning for an Unknown Future

It is interesting to note that only a third of our interviewees were using the services of a financial advisor or had long-term care insurance, and these were not the same third. There was some evidence in our interviews that these kinds of relatively expensive support services are only grudgingly utilized. Perhaps most of us are unsure if such services will be necessary until the moment of need and are unwilling to pay for them until that time. Nonetheless, some interviewees described their financial advisors as indispensable. They were grateful for their expertise, careful investment of their assets, and knowledge of the financial marketplace. Some voiced relief at not having to keep up with the stock market and other financial arenas and expressed confidence and trust in their financial advisors' know-how and effective investment strategies. We wondered how women of modest and moderate means could make use of such financial planning services in order to provide for their futures. How could women in all income brackets be introduced into this financial tool earlier in their lives? More financial preplanning would be helpful for women from all walks of life, backgrounds, and income levels. As innovative services are developed for baby-boomer women over sixty, financial planning should be at the center.

## Financial Worries

Our final questions about money were "What worries you about money?" and "Do you have people in your life to turn to about your financial concerns?" The majority of our interviewees expressed concerns about having enough money to last until they died. It is difficult, if not impossible, to anticipate all the possible crises that might occur in the future for which one might need money. Not only do our own possible health crises come to mind, but the health of those who depend on us—our parents, our husbands, our adult children, our grandchildren, our siblings, and perhaps our relatives and friends—is also a concern.

The following are just a few of the issues our interviewees expressed concern about:

- "How can we predict what kind of housing arrangement we might require or want?"
- "How can we know what inflation might do to our savings and investments?"
- "What will the stock market do?"
- "Will real estate lose or gain in value?"
- "Will a war disrupt our lives?"
- "Will there be a flood, hurricane, tornado, or other catastrophe that will impact our life or the lives of our loved ones?"
- "How much will a funeral, cremation, or cemetery plot cost?"

No one can predict the answers to these questions. Women will have to reach out to trustworthy people who have expertise in their individual areas of need for guidance. We all need to keep asking the hard questions and seek a variety of opinions. In our older years, it becomes increasingly important to maintain a broad network of contacts and recommended professionals in many fields so that we have a ready cadre of experts to turn to when the need arises. Even so, some of these questions will remain unanswered for quite a while.

One married interviewee in her late sixties shared her perspective with us: "Most women are scared about money. We're not prepared for being on our own. We worked hard and sacrificed. We saved, bought a little real estate, funded an IRA, and sat down with a financial planner.

We sacrificed early so we could live more comfortably later on. Now women must be knowledgeable about money and investments. It's likely that we will outlive our spouses, so we'd better know how to manage and invest our money."

Given the infinite number of questions we have about the future, it is amazing that close to half of our interviewees said that they did not have any financial worries. However, many said that they needed more financial information and would welcome more wisdom about how to manage money. They went on to say that they were concerned about needing an assisted living or nursing home facility sometime in the future. They expressed interest in various new housing options and wondered if they would ever need to leave their current homes or apartments. The questions persist and new choices keep arising.

While some were worried about their adult children's financial needs and capacities to help, others were interested in having enough money to be able to leave their adult children and grandchildren an inheritance.

Most of the interviewees described themselves as conservative in their spending; some said that they were very frugal. The latter took special pride in describing their spending habits that way, regardless of how much money they actually had. Their statements of frugality were more an expression of their values than a description of their levels of wealth. Still, compared to older people in other countries, even frugal Americans live rather well. Most of us have enough to eat, comfortable if not palatial housing, good health care and adequate health insurance, cars for transport, the capacity to travel, discretionary income to hear a concert or see a play, the capacity to give gifts to our children and grandchildren, and the opportunity to give to causes in which we believe.

Still, for each of us, money is a preoccupying concern that grows more immediate as we grow older. As we become increasingly limited in the ways we can earn money through work, we must turn our attention to how our accumulated money, however much or little that is, can earn more for us. Women's preparation for this activity is varied, but still relatively limited. It would serve women well were we to place a higher priority on money during our younger years so that in our third third we could be more financially secure.

We still have a long way to go in this arena to achieve not only income equity, but also financial literacy. Women do not want to become that proverbial bag lady reaching into a garbage barrel or pushing a supermarket cart down the street with the sum total of our worldly possessions in it. Each of us knows this woman exists. We see her every day on the streets in the downtown areas of our cities.

It becomes increasingly important for all women to learn about the inequities in women's work, income, and financial know-how. Doing so should push us to make sure that in our thriving country, women without means don't suffer financially, either in their early years or at ends of their lives We must also learn more about money—how to get it, how to keep it, how not to lose it, and how to grow it. We can do this, and we all should.

# CHAPTER 6

# Women and Health

**It isn't that I am afraid to die, it is how
I get there that concerns me.**
—Common comment by people over sixty

As we age, we focus much more on the state of our health. Perhaps it is because we notice our bodies talking to us more as we age: our joints creak and complain, our muscles ache more quickly and longer, our reflexes slow, and our medication list lengthens. Then we lose our keys and call our grandchildren by the wrong names, and we are sure that our brains have turned to mush. Even the healthy among us joke about physical deterioration as they notice others whose bodies are breaking down before their eyes. Chronic diseases seem to be all around us. We find ourselves having to care not only for our children, but for our parents and more and more of our friends who are not as well as we are. Soon, funerals seem to replace weddings. And though we have great access to information about health and sickness from the media, the Internet, and our friends, we are confused about what is good and what is bad advice. No wonder we fixate on being and staying healthy.

Yet it is a myth that to be old is to be sick and increasingly disabled. This myth began to be dispelled in the early 1980s, when increasingly positive studies in the new field of gerontology countered the notion that people beyond the age of retirement had outlived their health and usefulness. The results of these studies were especially positive news because it was becoming clear that the United States' population was aging rapidly. Fears had grown that our older people would become dependent on dwindling federal and health care resources. Concurrently, the ability to keep seriously ill elderly people alive and functioning through modern medical techniques burgeoned.

At the same time, the health and fitness craze to stave off getting older and weaker grew among the forty- to fifty-year-old population. Increasingly, people were living well beyond their seventies. Even centenarians were becoming more common. With these trends, grave predictions abounded about the depletion of Medicare funding and elders being left without resources in their time of greatest need. Although some feared that these forecasts meant the population would become increasingly sick and disabled, forcing an even greater social cost to an aging health care system already in some distress, many were galvanized into taking a more optimistic approach.

Gerontologists and philanthropists gathered research and studied the actual processes of aging, health, and illness. Some professionals were farsighted enough to assemble several scientists to conduct a long-term research program to gather knowledge needed to improve older Americans' physical and mental abilities and to promote "successful aging" in future generations.[1] The famed MacArthur Foundation Study of Successful Aging Group, made up of sixteen scientists, was formed in 1998 and conducted several independent studies funded with more than $10 million by the MacArthur Foundation over an eight-year period. The goal was to use an interdisciplinary framework to better understand just what effective functioning in later life could be like.

The outcome was the beginning of new knowledge about how people in the United States age, and many of the early findings supported "busting the myth" about nonfunctioning and dependent elderly. In fact, from the late 1980s to the present, the prevalence of precursors to disease such as high blood pressure, smoking, and high cholesterol levels has diminished as people take increasing charge of their own health and as disease prevention has begun to be a stronger part of our health care environment. As of today, the average number of disabling and mortal diseases among older persons has actually decreased. A greater percentage of us have our own healthy teeth, are more fit and active, and are more independent into old age, even as our length of life increases. So why is it that we still have so many worries about health issues and find ourselves talking about our health problems in social gatherings among our contemporaries?

The Oliver Wendell Holmes poem "The Wonderful One-Hoss Shay," mentioned in *Successful Aging,* by John Rowe and Robert Kahn, describes the sudden falling apart of a carriage, or shay, that had been intact and strong for many years. From working with many elders, it is clear that this is what many of us wish would happen when we face the end of life. We want to fall apart all at once, not in stages. New technology, medicines, and surgeries tend to "put us back together" but don't necessarily keep us functioning at a high quality of life. So the wish to either be healthy or to not live a long life remains primary to many.

## Dependency and Caregiving

Exemplifying this, one of our interviewees in her mid-sixties was clearly concerned that she would become dependent and ill, requiring daily care by her husband. She was not sure that he could provide this level of care or that she would want him to. Further, she had taken care of both of her parents long distance over a long period of time in their last years of life. She mused, "It was not my favorite job, as much as I loved them. I don't know if I could stay positive if my husband were very ill for a long period. As for me, I think I would just leave the world." She was decidedly distressed at the prospect of her husband or herself being disabled for the long term.

This was not an uncommon response overall among our interviewees. Several either had been or were currently in the care-giving role. The variety of circumstances and illnesses that wives were dealing with for their husbands or partners who were ill and required daily care, therapy, and management included heart problems (20 percent), arthritis (15 percent), stroke (8 percent), cancer (8 percent), blindness (8 percent), dementia (3 percent), Parkinson's disease (3 percent), and other chronic illnesses such as diabetes (25 percent). In addition, one woman had a handicapped son who lived with her and another woman cared for a mentally ill son who was in assisted living but was supported by her. One interviewee who cared for an elderly aunt and mother, each of whom was being treated for terminal cancer, summed up her day as "totally exhausting, without a thread of time for me, on top of struggling with the prospect of them dying and leaving me alone." About half of our interviewees were playing caregiving roles to their husbands and close relatives, while about half were not. The common concerns among all the caregiving women were health costs, the daily toll on their own energy and resources, and living arrangements now and in the future.

In the aging population today, we find more women than men, healthier middle- and upper-class people than those less fortunate, racial differences with more chronic diseases among races, and a huge discrepancy in how to make access to health care and health insurance more accessible given our large country and diverse population. But the window into the lives of older persons is often through the media, where the relatively tragic and dramatic stories are told. So we still fight the stigma of aging and the myth that to be old is to be sick.

## Expected Health-Related Body Changes as We Age

Perhaps it is the very uncertainty of the situation that causes us to become preoccupied with our health and its outcomes as we age. But there are things we can expect to occur, and knowing some of them may help us understand aging better.

Considering our individuality, it should be said, however, that common terms used to describe "normal" or "usual" aging are often misleading. While many of the physical changes we begin to experience are considered part of normal aging, they may also be signs of more serious conditions. Elders and their providers may incorrectly interpret these changes as normal, thereby failing to identify early signs of impending disease and leaving them untreated until too late. Additionally, not all of the "expected" conditions occur in each of us, and not all occur in the same time frame. We will be concerned here with what the majority of older people deal with in terms of declines and functional problems and those conditions that we found among our interviewees and small-group participants.

The human body is a miraculous thing. It was made to function under good and harsh circumstances. Additionally, it has reserves that keep us alive and functional even in our excesses and when sudden catastrophic events challenge us. It is not surprising, then, that continuous adaptive changes occur as one or more systems age more quickly than the rest. What we fear is that some systems will be overcome or pushed into the extreme and we will become ill. When that happens, the system's reserve is called upon and we adapt to the change without becoming ill. Our reserves actually rescue us throughout our lives.

For instance, our senses of sight, smell, taste, hearing, and touch all change slowly as we age. Although research shows us that sight and hearing change the most slowly, they affect us functionally sooner than the other senses. We know that smell and taste also change, as does touch, in our later years. But we often find that if we lose one of our senses, the others become more sensitive. This may not be universally true, but it speaks to the great reserves we have in all of our systems and the fact that one sense can provide increased input when another is not as sharp. For example, as our hearing lessens, we use our sight differently and more acutely to watch people as they talk and move. You can test this adaptation if you turn off the sound on the television set and observe that you can still understand what is going on by looking at how characters move in space and watching their lips, expressions, and circumstances. You are shifting resources that you may take for granted in a hearing world by paying closer attention with your eyes. It should be reassuring that we are good at recruiting our many senses when one fails us and we have a resourceful brain that allows us to interpret things whether or not all senses are working at 100 percent.

## Vision and Hearing Problems among Older People

Vision problems affect a large proportion of the aging population and often go unrecognized as an important health issue. There are many aids for those whose vision is failing. Increasingly, electronics are being developed that can provide better correction of vision or augment visual loss so that function can be maintained. For instance, there are projectors that enlarge and enhance one's computer screen so that it can be more easily read. There are also voice-controlled computer programs that aid either hearing or vision loss, and there are magnification tools either built into eyeglasses or for manual manipulation to improve or enhance visual ability or help people with altered vision. The media provides many helpers as well that aid both visually impaired and hearing impaired individuals, such as large-print books and hearing devices available at concerts, movies, and lectures. Many accommodations have occurred because of legislation to aid the disabled, and they have been helpful in making the public much more aware of the needs of elders, as well as younger people.

Falls are one of the most common determinants of disability, and poor vision is a primary cause. Deteriorating sight or loss of vision can render a person partially or totally dependent. In some cases, there is no known etiology, or cause, of the vision problem, and there may be no effective treatment. More research is clearly needed on vision problems among the elderly.

## Vision and Hearing Loss among Our Interviewees

Thirty-two percent of our interviewees mentioned that their hearing had diminished. It was not uncommon to hear the phrases "I have the TV louder now," "When I go to the theater, I use those infrared things so I can really hear what is going on," or "I know I hear more poorly…not ready for hearing aids yet." A few were wearing hearing aids, while others were delaying that decision for a while. We would anticipate that progressive hearing loss will become more common as these women age. They may eventually choose to be fitted with hearing aids or to undergo improvement through surgery within the ear or brain rather than cut back on the many activities in which they are now involved that require good hearing to enjoy.

A number of our interviewees were experiencing vision problems. Universally, they wore correctional lenses of some kind. Some had been diagnosed with macular degeneration or other relatively common problems of the eye in their older years. Cataracts were diagnosed among 33 percent of our interviewees; all had undergone surgery to correct this condition and the surgery had been successful, resulting in improved vision. The advances in cataract surgery have been especially impressive, and many older people see clearly today as a result of having undergone this relatively common procedure. In the past, cataracts caused many functionally sightless older people to become dependent. Fortunately, that is no longer the case.

## Expected Changes at the Cellular Level

Some of the expected changes as we age are at the cellular level. We don't notice these early in life unless they change our ability to function. Generally, everyday changes are in those cells that constantly reproduce, for example, bone, skin, nails, and hair, and we do notice these. But abnormal internal cellular changes can also occur. In cancer, some hormones and specific cells' reproduction speeds are out of whack. In diabetes, changes in pancreatic cells cause a lowered production of or insensitivity to insulin. These changes are not normal and can cause overt disease. Recent studies in molecular biology and genomics have enhanced our knowledge about early changes that may be related to a normal aging sequence.

## Function and Disease Are Not the Same Thing

Commonly, the changes health providers and scientists see as normal are those that most people over sixty complain about in relation to their ability to function. For instance:

- Loss of energy and recuperative powers
- Changes in sight and hearing that encumber function
- Loss of ability to move quickly through and in space
- Less ability to get things done in a timely way
- Muscular loss in bulk and strength
- More aches and pains upon movement
- Slowness when we expect our brain and body to react quickly
- Sleep problems

- Less ability to regain our expected health after sickness
- Feelings of inadequacy and loss of usefulness—a loss in vitality
- Inability to eat and enjoy what we are used to eating
- Weight gain or loss and inability to control it

Although our usual reasons for going to a health care provider are changes in our ability to do what we usually do each day in our lives, it is important to remember that providers are educated to look for a cause for the complaint, rather than the result of the symptoms. It is a common experience that many a mismatch occurs between what people are looking for to relieve their symptoms and improve function and the provider's focus on diagnosis. So it is important that elderly people talk about how the functions in their lives have changed because of the problem they present, and it is equally important that practitioners listen for the complaints that may alert them to a diagnosis, as well as paying attention to descriptions of symptoms.

## Common Concerns of the Interviewees

The women we interviewed, the participants in the small groups, and others we talked with over the course of writing this book were most concerned and frustrated with the health care system and how that system was or was not helping them make health-related decisions. Not surprisingly, complaints were very pointed and centered on the lack of time spent with the interviewees by their multiple providers in order to get trustworthy information. It was clear that outpatient visits were brief and often rushed and that explanations about what choices they might have and why they might choose one over the other were incomplete. Hospitalization or institutionalization proved to have the same problem of insufficient time.

In "Health and Health Care," an essay she wrote for Jerry Friedman's book *Earth's Elders: The Wisdom of the World's Oldest People*, Joycelyn Elders, former US surgeon general of health, provided insight into the problem of health care. She discussed changes to the health care system that would make it more coherent, comprehensive, cost effective, equitable, available, and friendly to both patient and provider. We would add that good health habits and preventive means of dealing with problems before they become serious or overwhelming are known to add positively to health outcomes and to a better quality of life.

In order to overcome frustrations with the current health care system, our interviewees were interested in taking it upon themselves to learn more about their health. When offered, useful suggestions were incorporated into their lifestyles with good results. They repeatedly asked where they could find good information. It is not always available. Additionally, while many good models of preventive care exist, present payment mechanisms, such as private insurance and Medicare/Medicaid, do not pay for much preventive care. Uninsured people have even less access to this type of care. This concern needs to be recognized in future policy decisions and dealt with in an apolitical arena that allows for new "out of the box" solutions to this persistent problem.

## The Small Groups: Health Matters

For the past five years, one of the coauthors convened and facilitated fourteen small groups of twelve to twenty-five women and men in a program called Health Matters. They ranged in age from sixty-two to eighty-five and were a group of highly functioning people. In the research definition, they were not a focus group—a group gathered to explore a particular issue in order to identify concerns that can then be researched—but they were a representative cross section of older people in the third third of their lives. Between January and April, they met each year from 2002 to 2007 for an hour each week to discuss a particular topic of interest. Since their facilitator is a nurse practitioner, they discussed the most recent findings and concerns that might affect their health and functioning. The facilitator chose several topics that had current new findings, asked the group to add to or delete from her suggested agenda, and facilitated a discussion based on the topics they identified. Notes were kept by the nurse practitioner to guide future programs. A list of their topics is useful in revealing the health concerns that many older people have. A complete list of these topics can be found in Appendix B. Some of the Health Matters topics were:

- Strategies for Successful Positive Aging
- Alcohol and the Aging Brain
- Abdominal Complaints
- Cardiovascular I: Blood Pressure, Cholesterol, Heart Surgery, Fibrillation and other Arrhythmias, Heart Failure, Implants and Valve Replacement
- Cardiovascular II: Drugs
- Healthy Lifestyles for Cardiovascular Regeneration and Maintenance
- Lipids, Fats, Vitamins, and Minerals—How to Know What to Eat
- Dementias
- Memory and How to Keep It
- Control of Type 2 Diabetes
- Stretching, Exercise, and Avoiding Accidents
- Orthopedic Problems
- News about Influenza and Pneumonia, and Immunizations for Elders
- Antiaging Potions and Scams
- Pulmonary Matters
- Getting the Best Rest
- The Up and Down Sides of Your Medications
- Walking: The Best Thing to Keep Healthy

The above list of topics resulted from suggestions made by the group and represents the concerns of the participants; it was not a predetermined set of topics imposed by the facilitator. It is also noteworthy that although there were many heath issues of interest to the small-group participants, they were in relatively good health and were active, well-functioning individuals.

## Common Health Problems of Aging

We were interested in knowing what the Health Matters participants, as well as our individual interviewees, thought about their own health. We asked our interviewees, "As you have grown older, how healthy do you feel in relation to others in your age group? What are some of the health problems you deal with, and how do you handle them?" While the scope of this book does not allow for detailed explanations of how the various organs, chemical changes, systems, and interactions among them cause variations of disease, it is helpful to present a picture of those diseases that seem most troubling to our interviewees.

Perhaps remarkably, a third of our interviewees responded that they did not currently have any health problems and were not taking any prescription drugs. This was one of the most surprising results of our interviews. The common expectation would be that almost all of the women in this age group would be experiencing at least one health problem. Yet it was clear that many had had health problems in the past with which they had coped and that these problems did not currently interfere with their daily lives. On the other hand, almost two-thirds of our interviewees mentioned having had at least one major illness recently or in the past. All those in this group were on some type of prescription medication, usually two or three, and many were taking in excess of ten to fifteen different medications. Descriptions of some of the most common diseases and problems that our interviewees and small-group participants mentioned follow.

### Arthritis

Arthritis is a joint disease that comes in many forms. There are over one hundred different conditions that produce inflammation or stiffness of joints. Together they are known as rheumatic diseases and have many different symptoms and causes. Most of our interviewees did not voluntarily mention aches and pains that might be related to arthritis. Perhaps they thought their discomfort was part of getting older, and generally it is, in terms of the wear-and-tear type of arthritis known as osteoarthritis.

When asked specifically about back, leg, or hand pain, a number of our interviewees described problems with their backs and with arthritis. They experienced reduced mobility and agility. Some of the women had undergone back surgery, others had had hip or knee replacements, and others were taking various medications to reduce the pain and swelling caused by arthritis. They were coping well, but were often slowed down by these conditions.

The Health Matters group participants continued to be interested in arthritis and other orthopedic conditions each year they met. They commonly asked things such as, "I can't feel my fingers in my right hand, and it is probably arthritis. But is it?" or "I have a bad knee, but it is getting worse. What should I do about it?" Since the group discussions were meant to bring out these types of questions and concerns, they were often the target for a future program, or if they could be answered then, suggestions for how to proceed with the problem seemed to help participants a great deal. One meeting about arthritis and orthopedic problems led one participant to say, "I never really knew how to think about how I walked since my hip started giving me problems. I guess I need to start thinking about it rather than limping down the street!"

Treatment of arthritis is usually related to treating the symptoms of pain, stiffness, functional losses, fatigue, anxiety, and depression. With trillions of dollars a year spent on pain relief, exercise regimens to maintain function, and surgeries to repair or replace worn-out joints, it is clear that people are looking for relief of symptoms that they know may come back because of the nature of the disease. Fraudulent schemes that promise improved function or reduced pain are often perpetrated upon elders. Scams account for many thousands of dollars spent on useless interventions.

Both rheumatoid arthritis and osteoarthritis make up the category of the number one disabling disease in persons over sixty, followed only by stroke and other neurological disorders.[2] The key to maintaining function is to be active without causing further trauma. A good diet and exercise coupled with social and interactive activities are the mainstays for keeping mobile and functional. Of all the symptoms of

114

arthritis, pain seems to be the persistent source of worry and discussion among older women and men.

## Chronic Pain

Pain is the number one reason people go to health providers for treatment. Pain is a warning sign, a subjective symptom that signals something is wrong and needs to be attended to. It is our early warning system and requires that we recognize, qualify, and report its effect to appropriate health providers, who more quickly know what the symptom itself might signal. Chronic pain is pain that lasts over prolonged periods and may or may not be associated with an identifiable disease. In those age sixty or over, 25 to 50 percent of self-sufficient adults and 80 percent of nursing home residents suffer from chronic pain.[3] Neurologic and arthritic pain are the most common types of chronic pain in older people.

Treatment of chronic pain has to occur using many approaches, which can include behavior modification, drugs, exercise, and changes in diet and rest. Using drugs for chronic pain must be carefully weighed against the impact of pain on function, possible interactions with other medications, the age and frailty of the person, and the person's ability to understand the dosing and management of the drugs. In short, it is a careful balance between help and harm.

Many of our interviewees and group participants were on chronic pain medications. However, many were also active people working to relieve symptoms from exercise and other lifestyle changes. They were always open to trying new approaches to living well with their pain.

## Cardiovascular Disease and Stroke

It is unlikely that those over sixty will escape change or disease to their cardiovascular system, such as:

- **Hypertension** – high blood pressure
- **Atherosclerosis** – artery walls thickening and becoming less able to contract and expand
- **Hyperlipidemia** – fat in the blood

- **Anemia** – low hemoglobin in the blood
- **Coronary Disease** – vessels on the heart's surface being clogged or stiff
- **Irregularities in the Heart** – valves that do not close or open well, large ventricles, or overstretched muscles

These are among the most common heart-related problems. But for optimal function of the heart, many of our other organs must also function well, including the lungs, which supply oxygen in exchange for carbon dioxide, and the brain, with its extensive system of nerve, chemical, and electrical connections. The heart alone is not the total sustainer of life.

Our interviewees reported few, if any, problems with cardiac disease. Since heart disease is the number one killer of women of all ages, even more so than breast cancer, this finding was surprising. Less surprising was that many of our interviewees were caring for spouses who were chronically ill with heart problems.

Women are less commonly diagnosed or treated early for heart conditions that lead to death than men, and they also usually show different signs of heart disease. With age, the prevalence of heart disease in women rises quickly to match cardiac disease rates in men. Women present with symptoms later, and their heart disease is more severe, affecting the statistics regarding death. So although women have similar prevalence of disease, they die more often than men with their first heart attack or vascular disease problem.

The Health Matters participants often wanted information about cardiovascular disease, lung disease, and neurological complaints related to vascular problems because many of them exhibited symptoms of the diseases. Yet many of the group participants and our interviewees were very active in prevention of heart disease. A full 50 percent reported doing exercises regularly, including 16 percent who said they swam regularly. Others went to yoga classes, while five were not only skiing and playing tennis, but were sometimes doing so competitively.

One amazing interviewee, Marion Downs, has made exercise and competitive athletics a regular part of her life and has written a wonderful book, *Shut Up and Live!*, about her approach to health in the third third of life. She has won several gold medals for tennis in the Senior Olympics, completed a mini-triathlon at the age of eighty-nine, and skydived from a plane at the age of ninety. She also swims, hikes, and skis. When we interviewed her, she was ninety-two and a half, had twenty-three great-grandchildren, and a second husband who was in an Alzheimer's nursing facility. She is often the subject of newspaper articles that focus on her remarkably active life, which also includes giving speeches to various groups and participating in some professional activities, a book club, and bridge. Although she has experienced various illnesses, chronic health conditions, and surgeries, she has taken advantage of many rehabilitation devices and services as well as medications in order to restabilize her health. She continues to set the pace for all those around her and is a true role model for positive aging and for maintaining high-functioning good health in the third third of life.

The majority of our interviewees were conscientious about preserving their health through exercise and physical activity. "It's a shock to my self-image to feel weaker. I feel so vulnerable, so I do water exercises two or three times a week," one eighty-four-year-old proudly announced. "I was ambushed in my eighties. Things caught up to me. So I went on an exercise binge," admitted an over-ninety interviewee. A mid-sixties pre-retiree was emphatic: "I'm very healthy now. I work very hard at it. I work out every day, swim, do aerobics, do yoga, and ride bikes. I have a trainer twice a week." Others reported that they walked regularly or played golf and were conscientious about their diet and eating habits. A few complained about being overweight. All of the interviewees traveled as much as they could and enjoyed spending time in the outdoors. Even those who reported fairly serious illnesses were continuing to travel, visit family, and enjoy the mountains and the seashore as much as possible. "We love to travel," said a smiling twenty-five-year breast cancer survivor. They generally considered seeing the world and participating in important family events as among the most pleasurable things they could do. There was a great sense of play and fun among them. These women's good health clearly allowed them to live independent, positive, and active lives in their third thirds.

The loss of health and stamina is the primary reason that many older people become dependent and lose their zest for life. Because health and well-being are so central to "positive aging," more needs to be done to incorporate regular physical activity habits into all our lives. Referring to her busy life, one mid-seventies interviewee stated flatly, "I don't want to practice for death!"

Stroke is the third leading cause of death following heart disease and cancer, accounting for approximately 175,000 deaths a year in the United States. It is the leading cause of long-term disability and the second ranking cause of dementia. It affects 500,000 people a year, with 400,000 being new strokes.[4]

Many of the neurological complaints of older people are related in some way to vascular problems in the brain or extremities. One of the group participants had a mother who was so impaired from stroke that she had to be cared for twenty-four hours a day. Care was better known as maintenance, with very little recovery expected. An infection or some other organ system failure, not her stroke, would eventually cause her death. The daughter was constantly stressed about making plans to be away from her mother because she feared her mother would die, and she felt guilty that she was not by her bedside continually. After describing her situation, she said, "I just can't do this all day every day. I feel so bad about that."

Another group participant was struggling with the aftermath of her husband's second stroke, which had dramatically changed both of their previously very active lives. What had been a life filled with travel together was now hampered greatly because of his physical difficulties. She was very concerned about his loss of incentive and energy, and she suspected that he was depressed. A great many of her activities were now centered on his schedule and the need to look out for him because of balance problems. She was often sad about the sudden change of affairs that the stroke had caused. She was impatient with the new, restrictive lifestyle they had while feeling guilty because she felt that way. Retired from a career in interior decorating, she had been used to both a physically and mentally challenging atmosphere. She missed the social life that had surrounded them in their younger days. The couple had a fine sense of humor and shared compassion and a good marriage, which was being tested. Humor and creativity have gotten them through major hurdles up to now, but she said that she felt she was constantly on alert for the next shoe to fall. Sometimes they both felt overwhelmed and discouraged. A new exercise program that included daily swimming and physical therapy helped them over the hump with promise for his future functional level. Their dilemmas are typical of many stroke survivors and their families and serve to illustrate how caregiving and many other challenges can become a large part of a woman's life when a husband or loved one is disabled.

In our group meetings, most (70 percent) of the people attending had heart problems and were guarding against stroke, heart attack, or heart failure. They were interested in preventive measures and what to watch for in order to prevent further deterioration, more illness, or death. Two women had recently lost husbands to heart failure after long illnesses, and one had lost her husband to a combination of stroke and heart failure. Many had cared for stroke survivors in their family or talked about friends who had been devastated by stroke. In the group, four women had already had major strokes and five women had either implanted defibrillators or pacemakers to prevent stroke, heart attack, or heart failure. Many needed to learn more about how to work with combinations of medications designed to treat heart and neurological vascular problems of many kinds, for example fibrillation, past heart attack, high blood pressure, angina, small strokes, peripheral vascular disease, dizziness, and fainting. Others who didn't have these problems were very concerned about how to prevent them. Additionally, many of the women worried about care of husbands and other loved ones who were not in the group but for whom they were responsible in some way. They wished they had known or better understood preventive health practices earlier and integrated them into their daily lives. Those women who had husbands and brothers with risk factors for heart disease often stated, "Boy, time to get after (name of person) for sure now that I know this!"

Interestingly, many women in the group had no idea that they were prime targets for heart disease and stroke. The differences between signs and symptoms of stroke and heart attack in women was particularly interesting to them, spurring some to go to their health care provider and ask about discomforts they previously thought might just be aging. In short, armed with knowledge, they vowed to be more proactive in the prevention of stroke and heart disease. They often had already put things into practice, but if not, they became believers and started. Perhaps they are the role models younger generations need to emulate before they become ill.

## Memory Loss

One of the most worrisome things to people who are aging is the possibility that they will lose their ability to properly use their brain. We often fear that our brain will deteriorate before our body does and we will be left in a world we no longer understand or can function within. We make jokes about losing our mind in the hopes that we will stave off any real deterioration. But it is rarely true that serious deterioration has occurred. Older people, given the same task as a young person, can accomplish that task, learn new things, and retain and use new knowledge with the same level of excellence as their younger counterparts. It just takes a bit longer, due to the fact that information processing slows as a normal consequence of aging cells.

Consider your young grandchildren, who can pound out all kinds of electronic wonders while you just hope you can get on e-mail and sensibly communicate with them. Then consider the fact that your brain has sixty-plus years of stored information and experience that may have to be sorted while their brains are much less crowded. Think of it this way: When your desk computer fails to act quickly, the IT person who fixes it may say, "We need to dump some of the information in your files and then your computer will work better." And, usually, it does. We aren't as able to dump files from our full "disc of life" as quickly.

Although women over sixty often worry about their brain function, most of our interviewees were not concerned about the present
health of their own minds. But they did wonder if they should be worried about it, what to do to prevent brain deterioration, and if they
experienced memory loss, just how life would be. To counteract these
concerns, some of our interviewees and group members had recently
attended memory workshops and most engaged in mental games such
as puzzles, bridge, Sudoku, and word games to maintain their mental
strength. An eighty-two-year-old interviewee mused about "losing it"
by saying, "So far I still see myself as competent. Not sure just what
I will do if I'm not, but for now my family helps me know if I need
help, and I still seem to know when I do too." But our interviewees
had cared for people with neurological problems and had found them
very difficult to deal with. Often, they did not want to talk about
these experiences.

## Oral Health and the Aging Gut

In 1975, two-thirds of people over seventy-five did not have their own
teeth. By 1986, two-thirds of the same age group had kept all or most
of their teeth. Today, people in their eighth decade have a remarkable
number of their own teeth thanks to fluoride, more dental providers,
and public health campaigns for good dental health.[5]

However, the mouth and teeth are a source of infection that can
be fatal, and this form of infection is preventable. The lack of preventive dental care for women of all ages depends on their ability to pay,
and dental care is presently not well covered by insurance. The general population has limited access to dental care because of a lack of
dentists in their geographical area. This is a problem that the United
States needs to address among women and men over sixty because of
its impact on health, morbidity, and mortality.

But the most common functional problems that plague women
over sixty are problems with the digestive system: food intolerances,
diabetes, cancer, ulcers, pain, elimination problems, weight gain or
loss, and lack of access to good nutrition. Many drugs used for arthritis,

bone care, pain, cancer amelioration, and increased sensitivity to alcohol or drugs can cause irritability in the digestive tract.

There were few reports from interviewees about problems with their intestinal tract. Most women cope with them without much comment, especially in older age groups, where speaking about digestive problems was often "not proper." But in group discussions and a more relaxed atmosphere, many jokes and anecdotes were brought up by participants during the discussions about nutrition, gut problems, and abdominal pain. Veiled comments about diarrhea, constipation, "heartburn," and flatulence were among the most common. Fear of bleeding, vomiting, "gut bugs," and mouth infections were next. Jokes were often made about these problems because in this age group they were subjects of social embarrassment and were not proper to talk about. Yet nutrition and the ability to maintain appropriate weight is a problem that plagues the older person from the standpoint of health, rather than vanity. Knowledge about it is important.

## Diabetes

In recent years, diabetes has become one of the most prevalent diseases in the world. Type 1 diabetes has an onset in younger years (adolescents and adults under sixty) and is usually diagnosed and treated much earlier and longer than type 2 diabetes. Both types are syndromes of altered glucose (sugar) metabolism (too much or too little sugar in the blood) coupled with vascular and hormonal abnormalities. Type 2 diabetes is more common among those over sixty, although children and adolescents are beginning to show alarming incidence of the disease because of obesity and poor nutrition. In the United States, type 2 diabetes is a major health problem, with an overall prevalence of 6.8 percent of the population and 16.8 percent in those aged sixty-five years and older. It is estimated that the cost of diabetes (both type 1 and type 2) exceeds $20 billion.[6] Diabetics also suffer from hyperlipidemia (too much fat in the blood) and increased blood pressure and have a propensity to put on or lose weight more rapidly than normal. It is not uncommon that people with diabetes of either type will have coexisting diseases, making management more difficult. The good news is that with proper control of blood sugar levels through diet, exercise, and drug regimens, poor outcomes can be prevented.

Although many of our interviewees and those in the small groups suffered from diabetes of both types, they appeared to function very well. This is not surprising, since diabetes is a highly treatable disease if one is willing to follow treatment guidelines. Our interviewees also had higher educational levels and incomes than the general population. Their segment of the population generally has higher motivation and resources to manage their disease, and more positive outcomes.[7] One of the most elderly of our interviewees (age eighty-eight) was legally blind from her diabetes. As impaired as she was, she had a positive outlook, was managing with help from her husband, and traveled with him. She said, "When I was young, they didn't have all the fancy stuff they do now for diabetics. I didn't know I had it until I was sick with my third baby and had to be hospitalized, but I must have. Now I do the best I can with my diet and medications. It is a blessing I am alive at all with this disease, so I thank the Lord."

## Osteoporosis and Orthopedic Problems

Fifty percent of older women and 15 percent of older men have bones prone to fracture with minimum trauma.[8] Osteoporosis is basically a failure of bone production to replace bone destruction at the cellular level. This results in changes in the architecture of the bones themselves. Bone tissue replaces itself actively throughout life. Osteoporosis occurs when the amount of bone tissue made does not keep pace with the amount of tissue lost. The bones most often at risk are the wrists, vertebrae, and hips, although long bones in the arms and legs may also be affected. In our mid-thirties and forties, we reach our maximum bone density. Following that, we need to pay attention to increasing our calcium intake, sunshine exposure (the sun provides vitamin D), and exercise to keep the bone turnover at maximum efficiency. Appropriate amounts of calcium and vitamin D intake can be obtained through dietary means or supplements.

Although few interviewees mentioned osteoporosis as a diagnosis, the Health Matters groups asked for a great deal of information about calcium and vitamin D supplementation. One participant joked, "From the information I have, I should either be eating chalk and sitting in the sun all day or [else] worry[ing] about kidney stones and sunburn and not mov[ing] so I don't break bones." This is an example of the overwhelming information available in the media.

With all of the media attention for over-the-counter drugs, mainly targeted at older people, conflicting information daily confuses the differences between fact and advertising. Supplements are a huge industry. The public has been drawn into thinking that if a change in diet or another pill will protect them from future disease or mishap, they should pay attention. Drug companies now advertise, which is a comparatively new phenomenon, and the required warnings in the ads can make choices very confusing. Relying on the media for information like this can be very dangerous. In the quest to find "the answer," people turn to health providers for guidance. A wise choice.

## Cancer

As people age, the prevalence of cancer increases quickly. Although many women over sixty are well aware of many friends and relatives getting cancer and dying from it, most are not aware of the rapid rise in all types of cancer among the elderly. "Cancer is a major cause of illness and mortality in older adults, and 50% of all tumors occur in the 12% of the population that is age 65 and older."[9] In women in this age group, breast cancer is the most common affliction, with colon cancer, lung cancer, and pancreatic cancer running close behind. All cancers, including brain cancer, increase in prevalence after age sixty. Why? There is not a simple explanation, but generally there are three overriding factors that may be at work: (1) many cancers, including lung, prostate, and breast cancer, may be slow-growing cancers that do not appear until our older ages; (2) having lived long lives, we have been exposed to more environmental carcinogens (cancer-causing elements) than younger age groups have, and they may cause tumors later

124

in life; and (3) the changes in our own bodies as they age (for example, decreased immunity, decreased cellular regeneration, chronic inflammation) can affect the rates of growth of cancer cells and the time of appearance of the disease. Other chronic diseases also mediate the development of overt cancer formation, as do the medications often prescribed for other problems. Additionally, older people are not as able to fend off complicated cancer manifestations as younger people, nor do they respond as well to treatment.[10] Although cancer treatments can prolong life in older persons, the treatments are often debilitating and profoundly affect the quality of life. This is not a statement to discourage treatment, but one of the realities that our interviewees and group participants recognized. A few who had had cancer treatment said, "The treatment is worse than the disease, and the worry even greater."

One of the major issues with cancer patients and their families is waiting for results and their anxieties about various choices of treatment. The unknown about the future is one of the most difficult health issues to deal with in any diagnosis. A diagnosis of cancer has often meant death. Even though that is not always the case now, for many it is still the truth they feel they must face. The question of whether or not to opt for treatment, and which treatment, is a huge one. It is never easy. So waiting for a diagnosis and then waiting to see if what you choose is working is tedious and stressful.

Often, the Health Matters group talked about family and friends suffering from cancer diagnoses and the impact it had on the entire family. For some, it was a positive wake-up call to do all that could be done to prevent similar types of cancer. "I learned that to stop smoking could delay death, but still, it does not stop the end from coming. But I stopped. It would give me more time," said one participant.

Many interviewees had cared for cancer survivors or had recovered from late-onset cancer episodes themselves. Among our interviewees, 35 percent were currently dealing with cancer or had dealt with it in the past. Their most common form of cancer was breast cancer. While one interviewee had not experienced a recurrence of her breast cancer for more than twenty-five years, another had just been diagnosed and was undergoing a full regimen of treatment: surgery, chemotherapy, and radiation therapy, followed by infusions and medications. A third interviewee had fought pancreatic cancer for five years and died a few months after our interview. Others had had some type of cancer in the past and were in remission. Almost everyone who had experienced cancer said that it was their most feared disease.

Many women had cared for spouses, family, or friends with cancer. These women's thoughts about the impact of cancer on their lives varied. It was clear that day-to-day living had changed dramatically during the course of the disease. Some were angry about the loss of freedom, changes in their employment status, or the expenses incurred, which they had not planned on when saving for their retirement years. All had learned that dealing with cancer required strength, courage, and taking what joy could be had day by day.

One interviewee had lost her husband to cancer only two months before the time of the interview. He had a progressive cancer that had lasted over five years. With a tremendous zest for life, they had decided to do the things he had always wanted to do, including traveling and seeing family they had not had the opportunity to see before. As he was getting weaker and more dependent, they used the time to plan for her future, to talk about things they had to settle, and to "love more deeply with each passing day." Able to grieve quietly but openly, she had found a great deal of support and strength in friends and family, which she felt allowed her to carry on and make progress with the things that needed doing, without discomfort to others around her so that she became isolated. Today her zest for life continues, both in his memory and based on her own faith, courage, and joy in life itself.

With the increasing number of aging women in the country and the fact that women are the primary caregivers of home-based care, becoming responsible for loved ones and friends with cancer remains a priority in the minds of aging women. The fear of cancer is only surpassed by the fear of profound loss of personal function in the future for oneself.

## Medications and Mishaps

The public is slowly learning that medications have both good and bad sides. They have found that new drugs don't always make us feel better and may make us feel worse in other ways, increase our symptoms, make us function poorly, or may be unaffordable. The reality that people will not take certain medications or will request a prescription change is becoming quite common. We found this to be true among our participants as well. When we asked the group participants why they did not take their prescribed medications, the most common response was "I forgot," and the second most common response was "They don't help and they make me sick." Providers and families do not express joy or understanding when elderly patients admit they have not taken what the provider prescribed. So many patients do not report skipping medications. What happens then is the provider's dilemma, a very perilous game of increasing doses of the same medication or adding one that might help more. It is the patient's downfall when either the medication that could help never gets prescribed properly or the patient does not take it as prescribed. Medication errors from either of these instances are common, even among those in health care facilities. It is a dilemma that all age groups share, but one to which children and elder persons may have the worst responses.

For women over sixty, help with medications depends on a good communication system within the health care system. Today, electronic storage and transmission of drug data among providers, pharmacists, and between pharmacies have made retrieval of records and dissemination of new drug information much simpler. The Internet has become one of the most accessible places for consumers to search for health information. There are a growing number of sites, often sponsored by the pharmaceutical companies, where drug information can be retrieved.

## The Health of Families and Friends

After discussions about the health of the interviewees themselves, we returned to an important part of our interviews, focused on the questions

"Are your friends and family well or do you have responsibilities related to their health? How are you handling these?"

As expected, there was a wide range of responses to this question. We began with the spouses of the 65 percent of our interviewees who were married. Many of them had lived through some periods when their spouses were seriously ill and required full-time care. Some of the widows, who comprised another 18 percent of our interviewees, had cared for their dying spouse personally, while others had relied on in-home nursing assistance, nursing homes, hospices, or combinations of all three.

Nearly half (43 percent) of the interviewees were responsible for other family members: aging parents, widowed mothers, adult children and their families, or handicapped adult children. While these relatives may not have been living with the particular women we interviewed, it is common in this age group for women to be caring for a family member or close friend. And some of the women we talked with were at least partially responsible financially for these family members and anticipated becoming even more so as their dependent relatives aged. This colored the retirement plans of some of our interviewees and limited the options that they envisioned for their own futures.

At the time of our interviews, the other 50 percent of our cohort had healthy husbands and did not have any dependent family members or friends. Most of these women spoke of having lost parents and friends. Some had experienced the painful loss of an adult child. So at some time in the past, these women may have assumed responsibility for others who were ill or disabled; they were simply free from those responsibilities at the time we interviewed them for this book.

It is clear that most women expect to assume responsibility for an ill or dying husband, partner, parent, adult child, relative, or friend during their lifetime. This goes with the territory of being a woman. Few of us are ultimately responsible only for ourselves. During the years after age sixty, we probably wait in more hospitals, spend more time at assisted living and rehabilitation facilities, visit more nursing homes, and attend more funerals than at any other time of our lives. These are the prices we pay for longevity.

## Thoughts about Future Health Problems and Living Arrangements

Since many of our interviewees and group participants seemed to be thinking about their present health, that of other dependents, and what the future might look like if they had to make new arrangements for living, we added two more questions to our interviews when it seemed appropriate: "What plans have you made for your own living arrangements as you are aging? What questions are vexing in relation to that?"

Most of our interviewees responded that they planned to remain in their current homes if possible. Perhaps this seems unrealistic, but all of our interviewees had thought about their housing options and concluded, at least for now, that they would prefer to remain in their own homes, even if and when their health deteriorated. Most of them had considered moving into smaller quarters, but neither a condo, an apartment, nor an available retirement community had appealed to them. One woman indicated that she and her husband would probably move to a single-story house from their current two-story home, as they anticipated future problems negotiating stairs. After looking at a variety of potential places to move, however, staying in their current home was the most cost-effective choice for most of our interviewees. In many cases, their mortgages were paid off and their homes were attractive, familiar, and comfortable. They liked them. "There is no reason to move," they said. Even going to another warmer location in the winter was not an option they chose, even though many could afford to do so.

About a third of our interviewees had taken out long-term care insurance. They had all considered it, but most had decided against it. Some of the divorced and widowed women had purchased the insurance, anticipating a time when they would no longer be able to care for themselves. Most of those who had such insurance had bought it when they were much younger and the premiums were more affordable. That's important advice to the baby boomers: if you are going to buy long-term care insurance, do it well before your sixtieth birthday.

Some interesting individual responses to the question about future living arrangements are paraphrased below:

- One interviewee said she would return to the country from which she had come years before, since nursing care was less expensive there. She had thought it through and said, "If I live long enough, I'll go back to my country. There's good care there, and it's not so expensive. My children's first responsibility is to their families, not to take care of me. I have relatives who own a nursing home. I could go there."

- One religious woman planned to go to her community's motherhouse, which is set up for retirees and has nursing and other medical services. "Our motherhouse has an infirmary. I don't need health insurance; we have a medical fund, plus Medicare," she reported regarding this unusual situation.

- Another woman, who was currently ill, said that she would choose to be in a hospice if her condition worsened rather than be a burden to her partner. "I've lived longer than they expected…I'll die quickly. And I'll get hospice care, if I need that," said this early sixties woman who had pancreatic cancer.

- A fourth interviewee spoke at length about what was not available in terms of housing for older women. She was mentally designing a collaborative community where each woman could have her own small one-floor ranch home, arranged in a circle of similar homes on a commonly owned piece of property with a community building in the center where all residents could take meals together if they wished, hold meetings, hear concerts, explore the arts, and enjoy socializing. "I plan to talk to my architect and developer friends to see if there is any interest in designing such an innovative community," she said seriously. We discussed speaking to other women who were alone to find out if there might be interest in such a concept or if there were any models of similar women's communities in this country or elsewhere. We were reminded of our days at girls' summer camps and of living on a women's college campus and concluded that we did, indeed, have some collaborative living models in our own lives at different ages. Would it be possible to create such an older-women's shared residential community? This is one new idea that deserves further exploration.

In truth, few of the women to whom we talked knew what they were going to do about their living arrangements as they got older. They had given the issue some thought but were not ready to commit to an answer. There were simply too many variables. And there was still lots of time, they thought. After all, they first had to move into their retirement phase, then they would think about where they wanted to live. There was still so much else for them to do. This was one thing they felt they could put off for a while longer.

## Positive Aging

Each person brings to the aging process a lifetime of adaptation, coping, and learning as well as circumstances within their family, work life, and environment that affect how they age. There are several theories about how people age.[11] Social gerontologists have coined the phrases *successful aging* and *positive aging* based on theories related to holistic health within and among individuals. Some definitions may be helpful here:

- **Successful Aging** – Rowe and Kahn describe successful agers as those who are able to live beyond average life expectancy with a high quality of life. This term describes a combination of optimal survival capability, health, and the experience of life satisfaction in old age.
- **Positive Aging** – Robert D. Hill sees this as being able to optimize the aging experience and make the process of growing older a worthwhile experience. Resources needed

131

include one's internal will, state of mind, the environment, psychological factors, personality, traits, values, attitudes, and beliefs that tend to be stable throughout life but can be used to cope with and modify one's own aging experience.

Theories are helpful in thinking about what might improve our present ways of dealing with our lives at a particular time. They give us new ideas. The authors cited all further expanded their definitions. In *Positive Aging* Hill notes, "[Researchers] suggest that although all people will experience age-related deficits in later life, there are qualitatively discrete groups of older persons with specific patterns of decline."[12] He delineates them into four categories: optimal/successful aging, normal aging, impaired or deficit aging, and diseased aging. Optimal/successful aging is described as "those who don't decline appreciably (or only minimally)." These are people over sixty who appear to have little or no disease. Normal aging is categorized as "those whose decline is typical for an individual within a given cultural group." The majority of women over sixty are in this category and are affected by genetic and environmental influences. Impaired or deficit aging is seen as "progressive decline that has not reached the diagnostic threshold for disease" yet impairs function in daily life. This group is characterized by people who present their health care provider with symptoms that prevent them from normal activities, but the symptoms cannot be properly diagnosed according to diagnostic standards of disease. People in this group are often treated symptomatically over time until the final category of diseased aging progresses to overt disease, "interacting with the aging process itself." These people are both functionally and physiologically impaired.

Erik H. Erikson, et al.,[13] called one of the latent intellectual skills wisdom. Wisdom also seems to be related to positive aging or optimal/successful aging. Optimistic aging encompasses the idea that function and learning change positively. As we gain years and experience some declines, we also gain wisdom and ability in areas of latent capacity. For instance, Hill speaks of wisdom as a quality "ascribed to those persons who are exceptionally good at learning life's lessons and then applying that learning to everyday living."[14] Among our interviewees and group participants, we found a large majority who emerged as wisdom keepers. They had the positive ability to view and change within the gradual declines they faced, and they were eager to share their insights with generations coming behind them. They exhibited a take-charge attitude and transmitted a sense that it is possible to redefine and reinvent our aging process to meet our individual goals, reach our aspirations, and maintain a high quality of life into our later years.

How does one achieve these positive and active attitudes and behaviors? The bookstores are replete with books and magazines to help us get and stay healthy. There are whole sections devoted to the physical, psychological, and spiritual aspects of aging and how to maintain a healthy balance among the variables of food, exercise, mental health, cognitive growth, environment, medications, and supplements to enhance our health. Writers, researchers, and practitioners in the health fields strive to show us how to keep aging in a healthy way. But there are many conflicting notions, and different sources do not agree. It is important to keep asking questions and looking for information you can trust, no matter where it comes from. Keeping the public well informed and providing accurate and useful solutions to health problems is not a simple task. Here are some approaches to finding sound advice:

- Sometimes we accept "expert advice" more readily from personally trusted sources such as family and friends rather than seeking several independent sources and making choices among them. Check the source carefully, understanding that not all sources are equal, no matter how loving.
- There is a lot to know about how a body is supposed to function and limited time to understand it. Seek well-known resources that make the concepts simple, yet present them correctly. Ask health providers what resources they use to answer their daily questions. Be careful of the Internet and use only well-regarded sites.

133

- When you adopt new approaches, medicines, and strategies in response to a health concern, consider the other things such as lifestyle, individual habits, and other body systems. For example, if you have had a heart attack, consider the rest of the organs and systems that the heart depends on in order to function and make sure you know that they are healthy as well. Often the treatments are complementary rather than additive.
- We identify needed "fixes" and adopt approaches that take the least time and promote success. Beware of promises that do not seem to make sense to you. They may not be sensible or may not produce the outcome they promote.

In our eagerness to help ourselves and take our responsibility for our own care seriously, we seek sound, believable, and tested answers to our questions. Basically, we want to know what works. It is important to look for strategies to help us define and address our own measurements of health and function.

It is impossible to give comprehensive strategies for all the readers of this book. However, both our interviews and our background knowledge made us bold enough to offer a few suggestions. We know that each person must search, plan, and follow through with her own strategies. The personal characteristics that help to develop strategies are:

- The ability to obtain appropriate resources in order to cope with age-related changes and declines, and then use those resources
- A personal interest in learning about simple lifestyle choices regarding eating, exercise, and problem solving that help you keep healthy
- Staying open to new ways of thinking about health and being flexible about trying to work them into your lifestyle
- An interest in focusing on positives to solve negative age-related problems

134

- Energetic and enthusiastic participation in what is happening around you, which allows you to gain new experience and experience joy
- The ability to change gears, helping you to move forward when difficulties come up

There are also some psychological barriers to positive aging to guard against and some strategies to help you improve your ability to age positively:

- **Rigidity and Negativity** – Seek out people and situations that are positive. Ask others about how they see your attitude, and if they think it is negative, adjust it. Replace negative and rigid thoughts with positive and enterprising new ones.
- **Self-absorption** – Bring others into your life. Practice being grateful for what you have. Ask others often, "Tell me about *you*," and then listen.
- **Excessive Worry** – Make a list of your worries and rank them. Think about *why* you worry. What is the worst that could happen? What is the worst that has happened in the past? If you can, "dump" the worry, as you would dump excess files when your computer is overcrowded.[15]

## Reaching Forward

Good health has four major components: (1) lack of diseases that cause us to lose function, (2) a certain amount of luck of the draw in what happens in your life and what your inherited genes and lifestyle values help you develop, (3) an attitude that lets us find new directions, and (4) the will to make change. We have little control over the first two components. The second two components rely on our participation.

Altering our attitudes and embracing change will make our lives healthier, more fulfilling, and as productive as we want them to be.

Author Jerry Friedman, in summarizing what he learned about the 110 centenarians around the world whom he photographed and interviewed for *Earth's Elders: The Wisdom of the World's Oldest People*, created a new way of thinking about our similarities and differences as we age. Rather than creating a portrait of aging that applies to us all, Friedman found a mosaic of traits among his subjects. In its simplicity, this book combines our commonalities while sharing a picture of how individual we all are. It can give us both direction and energy to look for our own living code in life and strive toward making that our reality.

Among our own forty interviewees and small-group participants, we found very hopeful signs regarding health: a substantial majority of them were quite well, while another portion of the group had recovered almost completely from past illness. While a few were dealing with chronic conditions, only a very small number were acutely ill. These were models of zestful women who had captured the essence of finding and using this time of their own to remain as healthy as they could be.

CHAPTER 7

# Losses, Regrets, and Gains

**If I had my life to live over...I would
go to more dances. I would ride more
merry-go-rounds. I would pick more daisies.**
—*Nadine Stair,* "If I Had My Life to Live Over"

When we think about the third third of life, we tend to think that our losses will exceed our gains. Even as we write this chapter, within the past twenty-four hours we have learned about the death of one friend from a heart attack, the rehabilitation of another friend after a hip replacement, and the continuing recovery of yet another friend from a cut on her leg that resulted in hospitalization for cellulitis. All of these bits of news were related to various forms of loss, were surprises, and none were actually planned for.

Perhaps it is the "not planned for" character of loss that disturbs us as much as the loss itself. We have been taught to plan, set goals, and strive to achieve them. We've spent the past two stages of our lives, sixty years in length, doing just that: growing up, planning and achieving our education, pursuing and launching our careers, raising our families, and planning for our older years. Then, after sixty years of trying to lead a stable and productive life, along come various surprises that we have not and could not have anticipated. What we haven't yet learned are habits and behaviors that are effective in response to surprises. We have not had lessons in how to cope with the unexpected. As a consequence, we are thrown into a state of imbalance and disequilibrium. This is neither a comfortable nor a familiar place to be.

## Losses

Some people react to crises in their lives with a sense of calm: they stop, think, decide, and then act in a cool manner. Others are prone to panic: they shriek, get confused, run for assistance, and often act in irrational ways. But most of us respond somewhere in the middle: we hear disturbing news, respond with some kind of emotion initially, think further, reorder our priorities, and then respond reasonably given our resources and capacities. Yes, we cry our tears. Yes, we are inconvenienced by the emergency. Yes, we wish it didn't happen. Yes, we must make new arrangements and perhaps spend money that we did not expect to spend. But ultimately, most of us shift gears and go on with our lives as best we can.

Some crises actually bring out the best in some people, compelling them to behave more sensibly, more generously, and more helpfully than they might have otherwise. They find strengths they did not know they had, draw on previously hidden resources, and rally others to participate and assist. They become more independent and competent, meet challenges in remarkable ways, are tested and meet the test. As a result, they gain in self-esteem and self-confidence, becoming people who are strong and admired. Somewhere in their backgrounds and psyches are lessons just waiting to be called up.

These kinds of latent strengths can be seen in the circumstances of war, when a soldier comes to the aid of their comrade who has been wounded. We call this courage. We often reward those who act courageously and view them as being brave, though they often deny heroism and insist that they only did what any ordinary person would do under similar circumstances. But that is not entirely true. Instead of panicking in the face of crisis, they summon their best thinking and behave exceedingly well. They may not be altogether calm, but they stay cool enough to respond in helpful and positive ways.

It would be useful if we all were trained in how to behave appropriately in the face of an emergency or loss. People in various safety and health careers are trained in this way: police officers, firefighters, armed services personnel, nurses, and medical personnel. They understand crisis and loss in very special ways that others do not.

## When We Lose Our Parents

When our over-sixty interviewees were asked about their losses, all of them spoke about their experiences of loss due to death. Most of them had lost both of their parents, although some still had at least one living parent. When a parent remained, it was often their mother, and they were spending more time with her than had previously been the case. One interviewee who had just turned sixty reported, "My eighty-seven-year-old mother and I swim together twice a week. We are very close."

Those who had lost one parent at a very early age were saddened by that loss even into their own older years. Their sadness reflected not having had the opportunity to know that parent as they grew into and reached adulthood. These women grieved cyclically throughout their lives as they missed their parents in specific family circumstances: graduations, weddings, childbirth, and other marker events throughout the life cycle.

In one instance, the interviewee had not only lost her mother during her childhood years, she had also lost many other relatives and her father had become an alcoholic. She had grown up virtually alone. And, having married late in life, not had children, and divorced, she was again alone in her older years. She had learned various ways to compensate for her many losses. She confided, "Since I don't have much family, I invested myself in organizations and friendships. I still do." Yet she was not depressed. In fact, in some ways she was more prepared for her older years, which she is now spending living alone, than our other interviewees who had not experienced many losses of those close to them. It was interesting, however, that compared to the other interviewees, this woman had one of the most extensive collections of old photographs on her walls. Her hallways were a virtual gallery of early- and mid-twentieth-century sepia-toned photographs. She missed her too-early-departed mother very much, and she cherished the memories of various aunts and cousins who had filled in the blanks left by her parents. Among all our interviewees, she would have to be considered one of the most independent. Out of necessity, she had learned to care for herself from an early age. As a result, she was not anxious about the current loss of her husband or her lack of children and grandchildren. She had learned to live her life alone. She said quietly and philosophically, "Most women balance their sense of loss with a new generation—grandchildren—that I don't have. I'm a loner more than others."

Amid the stories of the deaths of parents, one woman told a poignant story about her mother, who had been a paraplegic for most of her adulthood due to polio. The night before her mother's unexpected death, she had said, "I need shoes. I need my passport." Since she had not needed either item for many years, her daughter was astonished and urged her mother not to worry, but to go to sleep. She died in her sleep that night. One wonders if she had a premonition about her own death and her life as a walking person in the hereafter.

As with the interviewee above, many of us find ourselves in the role of caregiver with our aging parents. And in that role-reversal process, we come face to face with the fact that we are now "the older generation." We really do "become a parent to our parent." The following essay, written as a newspaper column in 1979, captures that dynamic.

Suppose your mother is slowly dying. The cancer is in remission, but the radiation and surgical therapies have left her unable to leave her apartment for more than two hours at a time…

Her once slim, stylish figure clothed in smart, tailored, elegant good taste is now a 95-pound frame wrapped in a variety of housecoats and bathrobes.

You can see the clavicle bones at the base of her neck. Her slim, shapely legs are now skinny…

The pain is episodic. Some days are tolerable. Others are unspeakable…

She, who never shed a tear, cries sometimes…

We work hard to maintain life; then we see its dignity, beauty and joy fade into frustration, suffering and frailty. It is not romantic. It is sad and beyond understanding…

Becoming parent to your parent. Mother of your mother—
loving, but helpless…

Suppose your mother is slowly dying…and the best you
can do is hang some new draperies in her bedroom or buy a
good piece of fish for her supper. Just suppose.[1]

With the death of a mother, there is often also the loss of one's
best friend. There are relatively few circumstances in which a mother
is not the most loyal and steadfast of all of our relationships. It is from
our mothers that we learn how to be a mother to our own children
and grandparent to our grandchildren. If our mother has negotiated a
successful long-term marriage, then we have a positive model for our
own marriage. If our mother has been divorced, we lack that successful role model and may feel more vulnerable to divorce. We may see
our mother as a failure, or, at best, a weak person. Still, we usually stay
close to our mothers and care for them when they become ill as they
have cared for us during both the sick and healthy days of our lives. It
is no surprise, then, that the loss of our mother is a significant loss and
leaves us feeling fairly alone in the world. If we are fortunate enough
to have our mother with us until our third third, she provides a model
for our older years that we either hope to emulate or react against. In
either case, the death of our mother is an important marker event and
is rarely viewed casually.

As women, if we were lucky, we may have had especially close and
meaningful relationships with fathers who were attentive to us and,
perhaps, even indulgent with us. Fathers often dote on their daughters,
encourage them to do their best, and reward achievement and good
behavior. How many of us have prized photographs of dancing with
our fathers at our weddings? Father-daughter relationships are especially significant in our formative adolescent years, and many successful daughters attribute their achievements to the self-confidence and
self-esteem that their fathers nurtured in them.

If, however, a daughter's relationship with her father was distant, cool, or even dysfunctional, the fallout can often be observed

141

throughout that woman's life. If these daughters do not find an opportunity to reconcile with their emotionally distant or hostile fathers before they die, there are often lingering regrets and what-ifs.

In one instance, an interviewee's father had left her mother while the mother was pregnant with her. That father didn't reappear until late in the woman's life. By then, the mother had died, and it became the daughter's responsibility to decide of she wanted a relationship with her previously absent biological father. In this instance, the daughter decided she did. The subsequent reunion was very difficult and awkward. The daughter, by then in her sixties, discovered her own daughters' physical resemblances to the errant father. She did experience some semblance of closure and gained some satisfaction of the curiosity she had felt all of her life. She did not regret having met her father, even though there was little positive emotional content in their meeting. It was sad to think that the father had missed so many opportunities to know his daughter throughout her lifetime, except for this too-late rendezvous. As a consequence, the father never had the pleasure of knowing his own grandchildren and great-grandchildren.

We tend to believe that it is never too late to mend troubled parental relationships. Then our parents die, and we never cease to regret the missed opportunity to make things right with them, whatever the circumstances might have been.

Although the loss of our parents during or before our own third third of life is not uncommon, it is nonetheless traumatic for most of us. It signals that the preparatory and dependent periods of our lives are over.

After the loss of our parents, we become the older generation. We are expected to know a lot, to be strong in the face of adversity, and offer wise counsel to others younger than ourselves. Sometimes we begin on a search for our roots as we review old photographs left to us by our parents. Some of us become master genealogists, travel the world for evidence of our families in other countries, or return to the neighborhoods of our youth to think about old times. Sometimes, as we go through our parents' clothes, jewelry, and other personal possessions, we reminisce and discover a tenderness and caring that we had almost forgotten.

One of our interviewees had been tracing both her own and her husband's genealogy for many years. They had even found ancestors in Europe dating back to the days of King Clovis in the fifth and sixth centuries. They had written four books for their children and grandchildren about their historic families, complete with photographs. In describing her attitude about this stage of her life, she said, "At this stage, I want to give back so much of what I received…This is a time to sit down and realize what you are leaving behind. What can I give? This is not a time to rest—it's a time to leave a legacy. It's difficult to do. It was a lot of work and expense…We had the time, so we did it."

## Inheritances Are Complex

Sometimes, as our responsibilities accrue for the disposition of an estate, we are either pleasantly surprised or disappointed about acquiring our parents' assets. In these circumstances, our relationships with our siblings can take a turn for the worse or become closer and more interdependent. It can be especially satisfying when a parent's estate assets allow the surviving siblings to work together toward mutually agreed-upon goals.

One of our interviewees talked about how the inheritance from her parents allowed her to work together with her sister and brother to set up a family foundation and give generously to many charitable causes in which they all believed. She had become the manager of the foundation funds, had learned to invest, earned interest and saw growth of the original funds, investigated potential recipients, became knowledgeable about tax law, and convened annual family meetings to make donation decisions. She had become a money manager and philanthropist. This endeavor brought her and her siblings much pleasure and satisfaction. In a very real sense, their parents' lives continued to be meaningful long after their deaths. This is a very fortunate circumstance.

The loss of a parent is often our first serious, close-to-home experience with death. We may be conducting a memorial service, making

143

funeral arrangements, writing an obituary, or viewing a dead body for the first time. We may experience the loss of a precious human being for the first time. As we learn to cope with this important parental loss, we are rehearsing for the many subsequent and inevitable losses that lie ahead. As initial shock and grief give way to melancholy, we try to stave off depression and loneliness. We may seek out a grief group, clergyperson, therapist, or counselor. We may turn for comfort to our partner, children, and friends. We may busy ourselves with the many after-death chores. But ultimately we are alone with our loss, and we must find ways to integrate it into our lives. There is pain in loss. But, as life goes on, we learn how to cope with our new reality and move on.

## When We Lose Our Partner

Among the eldest of our interviewees, those women in their eighties and nineties, the loss of a husband had taken a number of forms: loss due to death, loss due to confinement in a nursing facility, sometimes because of Alzheimer's disease or other chronic conditions, loss due to illness and frailty while still living at home, and loss due to divorce. Although all these situations are categorized as losses, the impact of each was different.

The widows spoke of grief and of missing their husbands. They talked of being lonely, but also often reveled in the positive memories of their marriages.

"I sort of accept it," said one of our eldest interviewees about losing to death not one, but two husbands. She continued, "When you're hit with something that fate imposes on you, deal with it, and get over it—close the door—move on." A second woman in her nineties said, "I was very lucky to have two wonderful husbands who gave me the freedom and the means to pursue my own goals while married. I was content to be alone these last years in my life because I had wonderful memories to make my life full, still."

Another widow, in her eighties, revealed her pride and pleasure in her long-term marriage by saying, "I'm terribly lucky. I've had a lovely life…My husband loved his profession; we were invited all over the world and he made my life very rich…I've always had people who loved me."

One interviewee who had lost her husband of thirty-two years to cancer nineteen years previously, after having been with him since they were high school sweethearts, was still teaching math at the middle school level at age seventy-five. The majority of her students were Spanish-speaking, and, since she was bilingual, she was an important asset to her school. She had returned to school in her seventies to complete courses for teacher certification so she could be employed in the public school system and have benefits, such as health insurance and access to a pension, after the required number of years of employment. She was the epitome of someone with a capacity for vocation and perseverance. She sold her large home and moved back to the United States from her lifetime home in Mexico. She chose to settle in a town near one of her grown children and bought a smaller home with her single son. Importantly, she reestablished her long-term teaching career in a new place, giving new life to her major career choice. She had been a healthy person most of her life and maintained an especially cheery and upbeat attitude. Her personal strength had allowed her to make major adjustments in her life and to weather the losses of both parents and her husband. She was a model of a woman who had been especially devoted to both her parents and her husband, and who remained in her same environment for a number of years, even though her children were grown and gone. It took this widow many years to shift gears and make a new life for herself in a new environment.

Another widow, who lost her husband of forty-two years fifteen years ago and "took a long time to quit crying," also moved to another state where she met a man who became her significant other and with whom she lived for eleven years. In contrast to the widow discussed previously, this widow was open to a new location and a new relationship. After some very pleasant years of living together that included travel, art, and golf, her second partner died. She moved back to her home state and has taken up where she left off: seeing old friends, making new friends, being close to one of her children and her grandchildren, taking classes, and becoming involved with the homeowners association in her apartment building. She is an example of a woman with exceptional interpersonal skills and aesthetic sensibilities. In addition to having a wonderful sense of humor, these qualities helped make it possible for her to re-create her life after multiple losses of male partners and continue to be generative in her work and life.

Another woman divorced her first husband only a few years after their marriage, remarried, and subsequently had two children. She expressed fear at the prospect of losing her husband. Both she and her husband had had a bout with cancer, and she was appropriately anxious about the fragility of their health. She was in an active search for wisdom and "future mindedness" as she transitioned into her sixties. She had taken up yoga, was now a yoga teacher, and was exploring the spiritual side of her life, having become disenchanted with the formal religion of her childhood. Her current spiritual search was also an antidote to her fear of losing her second husband, not so much to divorce as to illness. Sometimes we actually experience losses, other times we fear possible losses. Both emotions are real.

In spite of the variations in marital status, more than 95 percent of these women could be described as positive about their lives. They were upbeat and moving forward. Unlike the stereotypes of older persons who are preoccupied with their fears, disabilities, declines, and losses, we found among almost all of our interviewees examples of Robert D. Hill's concept of "positive aging." Just as described by Martin Seligman,[2] regardless of their marital status, most of our over-sixty interviewees showed signs of well-being, contentment, and satisfaction with their past lives. They had hope and optimism about the future. And they exhibited such "positive aging" characteristics as "capacity for love and vocation, courage, interpersonal skill, aesthetic sensibility, perseverance, forgiveness, originality, future mindedness, spirituality, high talent, and wisdom." Although all had experienced losses, they were not overcome by them. They had transcended their losses to shape new balances in their lives until a new, functional equilibrium had been reached.

## Woman to Woman Losses

The women who had lived their lives as single women without marrying relied heavily on their relationships with other women. "It's a loss to see friends age in a diminishing way. It's sad," said one woman who had lived her life in a religious community with other women. Among women who had lived their lives in a one-to-one partnership relationship with another woman, the loss of that partner closely resembled similar losses among married women. Although both these groups of single women had lost a number of close friends through the years, they were accustomed to fending for themselves and had established gratifying and dependable partnerships for shared living. They had made adequate arrangements for their own care if, one day, they found themselves in poor health. In the context of "positive aging," their strong suits were courage and forgiveness. Their losses included that of parents, siblings, relatives, and friends, which they accepted as a normal part of life. And they seemed to have an inner strength, perhaps for having negotiated the various phases of life on their own, or at least without a male spouse. It is these lifelong single women, in addition to those who were previously married and were now alone in their third third, who can provide us with models of independence in aging, despite their losses of partners and community members.

## Divorce

Loss due to divorce is often a lingering loss, especially when the divorce was initiated by the spouse. The result can be deep feelings of guilt, inadequacy, and failure. And with divorce, just as with losing one's partner to death, the prospect of growing old alone can be truly frightening.

One scenario is a familiar one both in Hollywood and in real life: an attractive middle-aged husband meets an attractive woman at a party or at a meeting, asks her out for a cup of coffee or a drink, and pursues the relationship until a full-blown affair results. One evening, he surprises his wife and the mother of his children with an announcement that he is filing for divorce. The wife is totally unprepared for this kind of a loss, fights in court for all the money she can get, is awarded custody of the minor children, and readjusts her financial life as best she can. The divorced woman, who has been out of the workforce during her fifteen-plus years of marriage, scrambles to return to school to complete her degree and takes low-paying retail jobs, the only kind for which she is qualified. Child support is minimal, and she now must find a way to earn enough money to sustain the kind of middle-class life to which she and her children have become accustomed, finish school, and start a new career that has the potential to support her and her family for many years. This woman is the classic divorced, middle-aged, single mom. Not trusting or enjoying men very much, she remains single as her children grow up. Soon she is turning sixty and entering the third third of her life. From her perspective, she has sustained heavy losses: her husband, her middle-class lifestyle, her ability to support her children properly, and the freedom to live out her later years with financial security and companionship. Some women never recover from these kinds of losses due to divorce. "My life will never be the same again," said one woman caught in this kind of circumstance. "I've lost everything we worked so hard for. It's humiliating, as well as sad. But there was nothing I could do," she concluded.

One of our interviewees, who had been divorced a number of years earlier, had a developmentally handicapped son. "He's my biggest loss. I think of it as a failure," she said unhappily. She was continually preoccupied with worries about what will happen to him when she dies. His reliance on his divorced parents, even as an adult, caused her to shy away from remarriage, to decide not to move out of town, which she would like to do, and prevented her from traveling extensively, which is one of her retirement dreams. Her concerns about having enough money after retirement have caused her to think about not retiring for many years. Even though she would like to work less, she thinks she cannot afford to. While she says she does not regret her divorce, her life seems to be frozen in time because of it. She seems stuck and is unable to move on. A major factor in her loss of marriage has been the neediness of her handicapped son. At this time, it is not clear that she will ever be able to transcend this situation. If it merely continues, then this phase of her life is likely to be inextricably bound to her son's needs and the inhibitions those needs impose on her.

A sixty-seven-year-old interviewee had been married for twenty-four years when her husband filed for divorce without previously discussing it with her. She had received enough of a settlement that her lifestyle had not been materially changed, and she had shrewdly invested both the divorce settlement and her income. The divorce did, however, color her feelings about ever being legally bound to another human being again. She said, "I enjoy people, and especially friends, both men and women, but I have learned that I did not want to ever share resources within marriage or a legal partnership again." She felt that it was not necessary to her well-being to have someone to relate to in a single intimate relationship and preferred the company of many people and her "own space when I am weary of company." Divorce had changed her perspective about both herself and her need for close compatibility to make her life meaningful and whole. Her financial status was satisfactory, and her life positive and active.

## When Our Children Divorce

Our interviewees' experiences with their children's divorces brought about some of the most heartfelt expressions of sorrow. One woman with four children had seen all of them marry, divorce, and remarry at least once. She expressed disappointment at not having been a role model for her children, even with her own very happy, long-term marriage. Then she recounted, with some humor, "We've had four children, and we've paid for nine weddings!"

Another woman, with five children, spoke of the disappointment over one of her sons' divorces, which included bitter fights with his former spouse over assets, and the distance she felt relative to her grandchildren, who were no longer easily accessible to her. She felt helpless to be of any assistance to either her son or her ex-daughter-in-law. For a woman who had sustained a long–term marriage and also led an independent and significant professional life, these foreign feelings of inadequacy were sometimes overwhelming. Her son's divorce had presented her with one of the few problems in life that she was unable to solve. "I am sad for my son and his children. But I can't do anything about it," she said as she summed up the situation.

## When Our Partners Have Health Problems

Even the women who still had their husbands were feeling loss due to the health conditions of their spouses. One woman's husband was in his nineties and had had a series of heart-related and other problems. He was increasingly immobile and needed daily attention. She had lost her daily freedom, even though she herself was relatively healthy. Other interviewees had husbands who had lost or were in the process of losing their sight and required constant care, transportation to various appointments, and assistance in the activities of daily living. These wives were also constrained in their daily routines as they remained near their husbands in order to attend to their increasingly dependent partners. Sometimes this meant that the woman's circle of friends began to shrink since she could no longer spend time with them, just at a time when she needed their companionship most. In referring to her husband, who had Alzheimer's disease, one woman said, "The worst loss is the loss of companionship in old age."

For one interviewee, the year that intervened since our interview had brought a tremendous decline in her husband's already failing physical health, but he had remained mentally and emotionally intact. In the process of providing increasingly demanding twenty-four-hour care nearly by herself, it was apparent that both her physical and mental health had begun to deteriorate. The bond between them continued to be extraordinarily strong, but the realities of daily care had exhausted them both. It was difficult for her to choose to relinquish some of the responsibility for his care to hospice and home care services. He was courageous and strong in helping her to do this, citing his great love and his need to have her whole and well when he passed away. Together they made the decisions needed to prepare for the future with dignity and love. They felt fortunate that they have had, and would continue to have, mental and emotional companionship even in these difficult physical circumstances.

With the poor health of a spouse or partner, our capacity for love is tested. If we can remain loving and caring, even through the worst of demands, both physical and mental, from our partners, our ultimate capacity for love will be revealed. It is this one-to-one, daily living partnership, perhaps more than any other, that determines whether we will have a time of our own in our third third.

## Loss of a Child or Grandchild

One of the most excruciating losses that a woman can sustain is the loss of a child or grandchild. The loss of a child in childbirth or early infancy can be devastating and influence one's inclination to have other children. Still, there are often many years ahead during which to recover from such losses. The loss of a young child or adolescent is especially hard, since that child has become a real person in our lives. Still, there are usually many years ahead during which to grieve and heal. When an adult child predeceases the parent, there is a special poignancy. The idea of unfairness for a life not yet fully lived pervades that circumstance. None of us wants to bury our child. That's not the way life is supposed to be. One of our interviewees who lost her middle-aged daughter said poignantly, "She was forty-eight, but she was still my child."

When a woman in the third third of life loses a grandchild, the loss is one of ultimate sorrow and brings forth a deeply felt sense of helplessness. Faced with her grandson's diagnosis of cancer, one of our Roman Catholic interviewees traveled to Rome and Israel to pray for him and for his recovery. It was not to be. His death at age ten remains one of the saddest losses of her life. "He had brain cancer," she said, "and there was nothing that could save him."

## When We Lose Our Friends

Among all the women we interviewed, there were reports of losing precious close friends. Very few women who reach age sixty and beyond have not experienced the death of some of their friends. Each is a different experience reflecting the special nature of each friendship.

My friend is gone.
I've lost my friend.

I thought I'd cried all the tears that I would cry...
I thought I was ready
But, I know, we're never ready...

My friend is gone.
I've lost my friend.

I will miss him more than I can say...[3]

The reaction of a woman to the death of a dear male friend with whom she does not have a romantic or sexual relationship may confuse his spouse and family. Not being privy to the scope of their relationship, they may feel jealous even as they grieve their loss themselves. Expressions of loss by the female friend may need to be restrained. Our culture does not have widely understood spaces for male-female friendships outside of the marital relationship. At times of loss of these male friends, we may be forced by various conventions to grieve in silence and alone.

The loss of a close female friend was a common experience among our interviewees. Almost all mentioned losing women friends and how these losses left big holes in their lives. Frequently, we spend time with our friends before they die knowing full well that they are in the process of dying. This is especially true when our friend has a chronic disease or cancer. If we are far way, we call often. If we are close by, we visit, do errands, and, perhaps, play nurse to them. A special kind of intimacy pervades the relationship. We are reminded of our own mortality, even as we minister to our friend.

We will all die.
We know it, yet we don't quite believe it.
Somehow each of us thinks we will beat it.

152

Not me, we say to ourselves.
Not me. I will be here forever.
Not me. Maybe you.
But, not me.[4]

When the time finally comes, we are no less sad because we have been expecting death.

It was 6:20.
The voice called us
To a white paging telephone at the airport.
I knew what the message would be...

She shrieked, "She died!"
And then we sobbed, together, hugging,
Tears streaming down our faces,
Stroking each other with comfort...

We had been lucky to see her yesterday
When she was still talking.
"I hope it's quick," she said.
"I'm so tired," she said.
"Just a minute, give me just a minute," she said...

And that was it.
By the time tomorrow came
There was no more talking.
And that was the last tomorrow there was to be.[5]

The death of a close female friend is a very hard death. We keep hoping they will beat the odds, survive to share another day. But, sometimes, that is not to be. And when death occurs, the loss is felt every day. It takes years for women to become close friends. There are so many casual friends, but really close friends are hard to find and keep.

...She fought to stay alive for four years,
As the cancer moved from place to place around her body.
And, it won, in the end.
It always does...
Our friend has died.
We knew it, but we didn't quite believe it.
Somehow, all of us thought she would beat it...

We were wrong.
And, now, for each of us
Life is a little more precious,
Time is a little shorter.
Mortality is just a little more real.
Death is a mystery that is just a little more familiar.
And, our world is a lot emptier
Because...our friend has died.[6]

When a friend, our peer, dies, we feel even more vulnerable. If someone of our own age dies, we wonder, Why not me? If cancer can strike them, why not me? If they could not win, even using all their strength and intellect, why not me? With the death of a friend, a peer, we become more vulnerable. And, perhaps, just a little bit afraid.

## When We Lose Our Own Health

After identifying various losses due to the deaths of others, our interviewees began to talk about their own personal losses, especially related to their own health. Those women who were in the midst of serious illnesses spoke candidly about the things they could no longer do physically. After a lifetime of outdoor activity, one woman with Parkinson's disease could no longer hike, ride a bike, or travel. She missed these activities greatly and had to make continual physical adjustments in every aspect of her life. She was fortunate to still have a very healthy husband to care for her, but she faced the knowledge that, barring a miracle drug discovery, her health would probably continue to deteriorate in future years. She is continuing to keep busy with regular swimming and exercise, as well as volunteer work at her local historical museum. But she is now often absent from social gatherings and misses her former active life.

As chronic disease takes its physical toll, so it has its emotional component as well. As in the poignant *Tuesdays with Morrie*, we watch our own bodies betray us and yearn for the kind of control we knew previously. It takes enormous courage to shift our body image from strength to weakness, from beauty to unattractiveness, and from agility to clumsiness.

Another interviewee felt acutely her loss of physical energy. She was slowing down and did not like it one bit. Being an artist and sculptor, she knew that her work required physical strength and stamina, and she worried that she might be constrained in the activity she adored most in future years. Her self-image was bound up with her originality and talent, and she was doing everything in her power to maintain those aspects of her life.

Another artist, who had undergone back surgery and an immobile rehabilitation, was grateful for her full recovery. She had returned to her jewelry-designing bench and was, once again, delighting clients with her innovative designs. She was swimming regularly and standing straight and tall. Then her husband, who had been her twenty-four-hour-a-day caregiver, began to have back problems. And then she was the one providing the physical support. Health problems had invaded their well-modulated lives. As a result, they were beginning to shift gears, reduce their social activities, and become more cautious in every aspect of their lives.

## When We Lose Our Energy and Our Positions

A number of interviewees identified loss of energy as a major loss in this third phase of life. Although they were not ill, neither were they doing as much as they had been doing previously. They were glad to have learned to say no to the many requests for involvement that came to them as busy and respected people in their communities. They were limiting the number of boards and volunteer activities in which they were involved. Others were cutting back on their work commitments or moving into phased or semiretirement.

A few mentioned the loss of work as a major loss. Some called this shift a "loss of function" and cited instances in which their personal visibility and their visibility in the community was decreasing. One successful career woman said, "I'm so defined by my job and community boards, I will totally have to redefine myself. I won't be anybody." These women thought that they were being viewed as less powerful, less influential, and less sexual. Most interviewees were a bit wistful when describing these kinds of losses. They recognized that others they knew faced serious life-threatening illnesses and felt a bit embarrassed talking about such comparatively minimal losses. Nonetheless, they were acutely aware of changes in their self-definition and felt a sense of loss not being able to sustain the energy, image, and significance of their former selves.

## Regrets

A regret is a special kind of loss. If one has a regret, one is sorry for something that did not happen, something missed that cannot be retrieved. Regret lingers. Regret smolders. Regret is water over the dam: done, gone, a missed opportunity.

Given that, for the most part, our interviewees had led full and satisfying lives, it is not surprising to learn that when asked, "What do you regret?," a full 12 percent replied, "I have no regrets." Even with further questioning and prodding, they did not identify any regrets. This level of satisfaction with life might seem unusual, or even suspicious. But for these women, life has been kind. They expressed that they felt very fortunate, lucky, or blessed. Overall, they were content and were taking advantage of opportunities and activities in their third third.

Some talked about things not yet done, rather than regrets. As if to say, "Before I go…," some were actively thinking about or planning to do those things not yet done before they physically or mentally could not: one wanted to get a degree in biology and was already in classes; two were going to write a book and said, "You've made me believe I can by doing it yourself!"; and one was going to enroll in flight school within the next two years, "before my eyes go!" They were not only now feeling free, but were pleased with the choices they had made earlier in their lives.

An equal number, 12 percent, expressed a few regrets:

- Not having had or adopted children
- Not having done something different about their marriage: divorced earlier or remarried after divorce
- Not having had a better relationship with their father
- Not having had a better relationship with their mother
- Not having had more friends
- Not having improved relationships with various family members
- Not having been better at parenting
- Not having spent more time with their extended families
- Not having done something more mind-boggling, like being a pilot
- Not having done enough writing about things that were meaningful to them so that others could benefit

The majority of these regrets are related to relationships, the others are about careers and being more adventuresome. It pays for others to heed these words. As the old saying goes, "I never heard someone on their death bed say that they wish they had spent more time at the office." In the end, it is life's relationships that count the most.

## Personal Regrets

For many women, marriage poses special challenges. While many of our interviewees were very happy in their marriages or had lost beloved husbands to death, at least 8 percent had regrets about marriage. By the time women have reached their third third of life and still remain married to the same person, there are few, if any, venues in which it is safe to talk with other women about the negative sides of their marriages. Humor often masks real problems, but it seems too late to substantially change a marriage relationship that has lasted more than forty years. After all, golden wedding anniversary parties are expected to be celebrative. Women tend to suffer in silence, perhaps fearing a loss of stature or embarrassment if their marriage is less than perfect.

Women should consider seeking each other out early in their lives to share issues related to marriage so that they might help each other gain insights that would prevent so many regrets later on. Marriage, and the challenges and problems associated with it, are not always discussed, even between best friends. Then, when problems increase and keeping conflicts secret is no longer possible, it may be too late and divorce may be the only option. On the other side of the coin, divorce may be the best solution, and women need to be able to reach that conclusion reasonably and not risk losing face or their relationships with others.

Waiting until the third third of life to solve internal marriage problems is not very wise. A number of years ago, in the context of the women's movement and before so many women were working full time, it was commonplace to belong to a women's group or coffee klatch, an informal gathering of women of similar ages who met regularly to talk about their children and families. One such group of suburban friends met on Saturday mornings while the husbands took care of the children. Another group of neighbors met over bridge games in the evening while the husbands babysat. Today, since young mothers are also often working, weekends and evenings usually belong to the family. Now that the sewing circles, quilting bees, and consciousness-raising groups are no more, when can young women meet to share and learn from one another? Or, better yet, when can intergenerational groups of women get together to discuss personal matters and have a venue where younger women can learn from older and, hopefully, wiser women? There is an unmet need in this area, but small glimmers are beginning to appear in the form of intentional luncheons including women of diverse ages. Rather than inviting a speaker for an expert lecture on a particular subject, women of various ages are beginning again to gather around luncheons or small dinners to get to know one another better. As these groups stabilize and schedule repeated events, a new round of conversations between generations of women is likely to occur. These efforts will seed new relationships and friendships, which can be one answer to the current identified need for intimacy in our increasingly impersonal society.

## Regrets about Relationships and Behavior

A full quarter of our interviewees regretted aspects of their own behavior in relationship to others. They said things such as:

- "I was too unforgiving."
- "I was too severe."
- "I was too judgmental."
- "I was too impatient with my children."
- "I was too hard on my employees."
- "Sometimes I wasn't fair."
- "I was too self-involved."
- "I should have been kinder."
- "I should have done more for others."

These women were relatively self-critical and wished they had been kinder and gentler in their dealings with others. No one regretted being too nice and wished they had been more stern. The lesson here is that when we have a choice, we should choose our softer selves over our more demanding selves. It pays to give people the benefit of the doubt. We like ourselves better when we are nicer people. And we are less likely to burn bridges if we use the more generous and loving parts of ourselves.

The second lesson here is to try to pay better attention to our relationships with friends and family throughout our lives so that we don't carry regrets with us into our older years, when we may not have an opportunity to patch up or retrieve lost relationships.

## Regrets about Education and Careers

The two areas in which more than a quarter of our interviewees had regrets were education and careers. In regard to education, interviewees regretted that they did not go on in school and complete the next degree. In some cases, they wished they had started college earlier in their lives. In most cases, however, they regretted not having completed a doctorate or other graduate degree. One woman regretted that she had not urged her children to pursue more education in order to have the opportunity for more lucrative careers than they actually had. Fortunately, today it is possible to return to school as an adult student at almost any age, even after age sixty. So this regret has the potential to be rectified, even in the third third of our lives.

The largest number of expressed regrets regarded careers. Some of the interviewees said that they wished they had pursued different careers than the ones they had chosen. For the most part, the alternative careers that were mentioned were demanding, professional, and required extensive education: airline pilot, politician, architect, or a career in medicine. The general gist of these remarks was that these women, many of whom were young adults during the women's movement of the 1970s, wished they had started on their career paths earlier, been more ambitious about their career goals, and pursued higher levels of education. The clear message to their daughters and to the women they mentor is to set out on a career path early, gain as much education as possible, and be ambitious about the career you consider.

It is also clear that these women greatly valued their marriages and families. No one regretted having children; some regretted not having more. And almost all the interviewees talked in detail about the families from which they came as well as the families they had established themselves. This group, now in their later years, believed strongly that women can indeed have it all, although maybe not all at the same moment in time. Their regrets were more about what they had not done than what they had done. This is an important commentary on the lives of women in the second half of the twentieth century and the beginning of the twenty-first century.

## Regrets about Bodies and Art

Another small number of our interviewees said that they wished they had started exercise earlier in their lives and taken better care of their bodies, while others wished they had been more artistic and creative. Members of this small group expressed regret that their bodies were not as agile and mobile as they once were. They regretted having to give up physical activities that they enjoyed, and expressed a bit of nostalgia for the good looks and good physical coordination of their youth. However many of these women over sixty were still skiing, playing tennis, riding their bikes, swimming, and hiking. *And* this was even true for some in their eighties and nineties.

## Gains

Our interviewees actually spent more time talking about the gains of this period of life than they did about their losses and regrets. Most of them saw the glass as half full, not half empty. With amazing resilience, they described all that they had gained, especially during their third third.

### We Gain Grandchildren

First among their enthusiasms were grandchildren. Not everyone was a grandmother, but 70 percent were. Some had step-grandchildren and others already had great-grandchildren. Some had so many grandkids, they could hardly remember all their names. Some had grandchildren scattered all over the country and the world. They organized their time around getting to see them as often as possible. They traveled far and wide for births, birthdays, family reunions, Christmas, Easter, bar and bat mitzvahs, graduations, and weddings. Nothing gave them more joy. One interviewee described the third third as "the culmination of life." Her major gain was her pride in her grandchildren, which, to her, were evidence of the concept of culmination.

### We Gain Freedom

The second most frequently mentioned gain at this time of life was freedom, for example:

161

- The freedom to do what you want to do
- The freedom from responsibilities of work and dependent children
- The freedom to say what you mean without worrying about what others think
- The freedom that comes from a lifetime of building self-confidence

A very content interviewee said, "To me, my gains mean freedom. I'm liberated to do whatever I want to do. I have more experience, more confidence, and I've made more emotional and spiritual gains. I'm nicer now, more relaxed. It's a very good time. I give thanks."

This freedom to be who one really is was voiced by almost all the interviewees as an important gain in this period of life. These women now speak their minds without fear of reprisal. They take positions on issues with the confidence born of experience. They choose how they wish to spend their time and with whom to spend it. Like the Red Hat Society, they wear hats and outrageous clothes if they want to. They have given away their business suits and high heels. They are free to spend each day as they choose. They sleep late in the morning. They stay up late at night. This kind of freedom is an enormous gain, especially for women who grew up at a time when the culture defined women's roles so narrowly. Today, these women are enjoying their most important gain: the freedom to be who they really are.

## We Gain Deeper Relationships

The third set of gains was in relationships. Interviewees mentioned the maturation of their relationships with their spouses and friends. These relationships were deeper and richer, and there was more free time during which to nurture them. Interviewees were more relaxed and described themselves as more gentle and more confident. There was now more time for travel, lunch, long chats on the phone, and sharing ideas than when the demands of work and family were primary. Some women said that they were simply having a good time.

## We Gain a Time of Our Own

Many of the women we interviewed had gained what they called "give back time." Some who went to college on scholarships had established scholarships for others. Some had become generous philanthropists. Others were serving on nonprofit boards and giving of their professional talents without compensation. Others were giving back by mentoring younger women and teaching them the skills they had developed over a lifetime. Some were still teaching, whether in formal or informal groups, to both older and younger women, and they described "giving back" in that way.

One interviewee said, "The gains at this time of life are enormous." Then she cited her successful life, including meaningful work, family, prominence, achievements, children, grandchildren, financial security, and good health after having lived for more than twenty-five years following a bout with breast cancer. Clearly, she had it all. But most important to her now was "the privilege of slowing down." She felt that she and her husband had earned the right to stop and smell the roses. They had worked hard, raised their family, served the community, and now it was their turn. Others echoed this positive view, calling it "feeling comfortable," having no "down time," "taking time for family and friends," and "having an opportunity to refocus our energies toward that which we truly care about." There was a no-nonsense tone to these citations of gains. The interviewees were thoughtful and serious about the opportunities this time of life afforded them. They had worked hard and long and felt that they deserved to shift gears into a time of their own.

## We Gain Our True Selves

Finally, everyone spoke of gains unrelated to the use of time, gains in their own inner development. They felt they had gained wisdom, not just knowledge. They had gained patience, not just tolerance. They had gained maturity, not just age. They had gained personal memory, not just history. And they had gained judgment, not just information. In many ways, these women over sixty were justifiably proud of their accomplishments but not captive to a need for recognition. They had already experienced success in their careers and received recognition from their communities and the love and respect of their families. They could now relax and savor all that they had accumulated and achieved.

By way of summary, the most often cited gains of the third third of life are:

- The blessings of grandchildren
- The freedom to be yourself
- Deeper relationships with family members and friends
- Time of one's own
- Inner development

By all measures, it is a good time, this third third. These women had negotiated the swirling rapids of life, righted their boats, and were now sailing smoothly toward their destinations. Their journeys had not been easy, but neither were they impossible. On balance, they had arrived at age sixty and beyond with positive attitudes, pride in their achievements, energy for new activities, and optimism about the future. In Erik H. Erikson's terms, they were being generative and not falling prey to stagnation.[7] In this third third, there were clearly more gains than losses and regrets. And, indeed, life was good.

# CHAPTER 8

# From Generation to Generation

**Sometimes, when you listen closely,
you can hear the future.**
—Shell Oil Advertisement, *Rocky
Mountain News*, July 7, 2007

## Introduction

Now that there are more than 36.8 million people in the United States over sixty-five and the huge generation of 78 million baby boomers, born between 1946 and 1964, began to turn sixty in 2006, everyone has become increasingly interested in these older age groups. You can see it in the television commercials for prescription medicines and over-the-counter drugs and in newspaper advertisements for retirement housing. You can hear it on radio advertisements and in discussions of financial products. You can find it in the bookstores in expanding retirement sections. You can read it in magazine articles analyzing the impact of this demographic shift on everything from business to housing to the workplace to the federal budget. There are new websites that cater to this older population, free high-quality dinners offered to the public that are designed to attract investors, an increasing number of retirement communities with many housing options, and more intergenerational movies. Even retail stores are beginning to carry more women's clothing for those of us beyond the junior or petite category. Imagine, we are finally beginning to be taken seriously as a significant and influential demographic group. In fact, it is predicted that by 2010, there will be 40 million people over sixty-five and by 2020, 55 million people will be sixty-five and older. The group of elderly over eighty-five is projected to grow by 40 percent between 2000 and 2010, from 4.2 million to 6.1 million, according to AARP. Women will be the majority of those older Americans, based on the fact that in 2005, there were

21.4 million older women compared with 15.4 million older men.[1]

But while there is increased attention to both aging men and women, few have yet realized that it is women between sixty and ninety, and even beyond, who have set the pace and can provide the role models for those who will follow, especially the baby boomers. In this chapter, we will examine the relationships between these two groups that are now converging in the third thirds of their lives, and we will review what we have heard and learned from our interviewees regarding what they want to tell the baby boomers who are following them.

People around the world are living longer, more active, healthier lives than ever before in history. But we have yet to develop sufficient arenas for discussion that reflect on and provide for an exchange of ideas among women over sixty. Perhaps we need women's Third-Third Transition (TTT) workshops, seminars, and discussion groups where women can explore a number of lifestyle and activity choices among peers who are facing similar challenges. Recall that during the women's movement women developed consciousness-raising groups that met regularly, were often intergenerational, and provided the participants with ideas and personal support while they were making difficult changes in their personal and public lives. Those groups give us one model for the kinds of TTT groups that could be developed now.

In this Internet age, we can anticipate the wider development of various websites and blogs addressed to people in the third third of their lives. Some combination of one-to-one, group, and electronic communications and support is likely to emerge. Perhaps there will be private support for these new ventures through foundations, health insurance companies, financial management firms, hospitals, or senior housing businesses. Or perhaps in the public sector, state public health departments, state departments of labor, or local health departments will realize that their health prevention and grassroots efforts would be enhanced if they focused on wellness and on the psychological support needed by those over sixty. We eagerly anticipate the birth of these new services, as the "market" of men and women over sixty increases and their needs and interests become central to society.

But first, we need a new way of viewing the relationship between the baby boomers and the Greatest Generation.

## A Brief Historical Perspective

Various population groups are referred to as follows:

- Those born between 1900 and 1922 are called the turn-of-the-century or the World War I generation.
- Those born between 1923 and 1945 are referred to as the Depression-era generation, the World War II generation, and the Greatest Generation.[2]
- Those born between 1946 and 1964 are the baby boomers, products of the post–World War II economic boom.
- Those born between 1965 and 1982 are called the baby busters or Generation X.
- Those born between 1983 and 2000 are the Echoes or the Millennial generation.

There are certain characteristics and values that have been attributed to each of the above groups by writers and researchers, thereby influencing planners and marketers. If we accept these generalizations and descriptors, we can see why there may be conflicts or a lack of understanding between age groups in the workplace, in academia, and in the political arena. A brief look at history and values across generations reveals that, in general:

- The World War I generation has been shaped mainly by communities with small neighborhood businesses, an agricultural family model, waves of new immigrants, and traditional roles for males and females.
- The Depression-era/Greatest Generation knew poverty personally during the Depression, supported our country, and won World War II. They remain very patriotic, value work, have developed large and successful corporations,

and have been comfortable with centralization, both in business and in government. This is the generation that powered the mightiest hierarchical military that the world has ever known, in World War II, and returned home to build the largest and most successful highly centralized corporations in the world. As young-adult change agents, they fought for social justice in the civil rights movement, the independence and equality of women in the women's movement, and were split on America's role in the world during the Korean and Vietnam wars, as well as being divided on other key domestic and international issues during all the years that have followed.

- The baby boomers have long understood that their numbers give them a high level of influence, and they have brought their values into the workplace and politics. They appreciate decentralization, are conscious of the environment, use technology comfortably, value short-term satisfaction, and have had the benefit of a relatively materialistic and affluent lifestyle. They have always lived in the midst of deep divisions in our society.

- Generation X, sometimes called the baby busters, number fewer than half of the boomers and have been early adopters of technology, accept centralization once again, are accustomed to living among diverse values and political debates, and seek personal satisfaction in their work. This post–baby boomer group has less influence over social norms, due to their smaller numbers and fewer protest ideologies. They reached young adulthood when our country was becoming more affluent and conservative, and were inclined to be climbing career ladders and taking advantage of the gains made by their predecessors.

- The youngest group, now being referred to as the Echoes or the Millennials, are about the same size group as the baby boomers, are still students or are beginning their careers, have grown up with technology, and have never known a time when the United States was not involved in a controversial war on foreign soil. They are distinguished especially by their technological expertise and their frequent disdain for those older than they who are not as expert with new technologies. Their cell phones are always on their ear or in the pocket of their hoodie. These are the grandchildren and great-grandchildren of women over sixty, now in the third third of their lives.

Yes, these are generalizations and do not characterize everyone in each group. But in general, these descriptors remind us that: (1) we are all products of the times in which we are born and live; (2) we are influenced by those around us and the economic and political conditions of our times; and (3) change is a constant as our lives and our world continue to evolve.

## Women of the Greatest Generation

Most of the women interviewed for this book are part of the Depression-era/Greatest Generation, having been born between 1923 and 1945. A few interviewees belong to other generations: those just turning sixty are part of the baby-boomer group and those in their late eighties and early nineties belong to the World War I generation. The age distribution of our over-sixty interviewees looks like a bell curve. Nonetheless, a few years often make a big difference.

When we think of the Greatest Generation, most of us picture the surprise attack on Pearl Harbor, the D-Day landing at Normandy in France, the London Blitz, the freezing Russian offensive, the Bataan Death March, the Holocaust and the Nazi concentration camps, the dropping of atomic bombs on Hiroshima and Nagasaki in Japan—all scenes of men at war. When these events were happening, where were the women of the Greatest Generation?

Only twelve women (24 percent) out of a total of fifty people were profiled in Tom Brokaw's book *The Greatest Generation*. During World

War II, many women were following their men from camp to camp within the United States or waiting for them to return from overseas assignments. Some were USO (United Service Organizations) volunteers, others were volunteer air-raid wardens, and some volunteered for the Red Cross, rolling bandages and serving coffee and donuts to servicemen on troop trains. A few of our interviewees were old enough to have been in the service themselves: the WAVES, the WACs (Women's Army Corps), or the WAFs (Women in the Air Force). Several served as pilots, nurses, and civilian health volunteers. In short, they were on the front lines, just like the men of the same era, but their stories are not as well known.

Whether we were young adults, teenagers in high school, or kids in elementary school, the war made a big difference in our lives and in our psyches. We developed a love of country not seen since those World War II years. For many, that devotion to America later translated into political activism: local political party activities, League of Women Voters memberships, participation in the civil rights movement, and leadership in the women's movement. Some have even called this group "the aging Feminine Mystique Generation,"[3] since they were so heavily influenced by Betty Friedan's 1963 book *The Feminine Mystique*, which provided much of the rationale for the women's movement.

A key feature of this group of women is their deep-seated values, rooted in having spent their formative years during World War II. Those values include self-reliance, independence, responsibility for family, love of country, and deep commitments to causes that led to working with others to achieve common goals. These values have translated into their work at home and in the workplace; their volunteer service to their communities, their churches, and their organizations; and their interests in lifelong learning. They are now defining their later years and retirement lifestyles around these values, just as they defined the busy middle years of their lives around them. These are the women who, after all, simultaneously raised their children, returned to school, and went back to work. They juggled the hours of every day so that they could have it all, even if they couldn't have it all at the same time. They were the pioneers who emerged from the women's movement, changed the workplaces of America, and raised the baby boomers and Gen Xers of today's technology-based society.

These are pretty remarkable women who have been given little praise for their efforts, and their creative and courageous life stories have literally achieved a revolution in our society. Not everyone marched in protests or challenged college entrance quotas. But in millions of silent and quiet ways, they gave birth to a new social ethic: equality in public life, equity in private life. They ran for political office and smashed glass ceilings in the workplace. They shared household chores with their husbands and brought more daddies into the daily lives of their children. These strong women have a new vision and model of what a woman's life can be in the twenty-first century: both feminine and feminist, both mothers and managers, both grandmas and innovators. These are the women that this book celebrates.

## The Greatest Generation Women and the Baby Boomers

There are many interesting and unprecedented ways in which the Greatest Generation women relate to the baby boomers. Given that Greatest Generation women are still healthy and active well past age sixty, this may be the first time in history when two adult generations of very different values and backgrounds have simultaneously functioned in public community arenas, workplaces, and private households. For many, this means that the women in these two groups are not only mother and daughter, but they may also be colleagues at work and volunteers on the same community committees. In truth, they are peers, although they may be from very different generations, backgrounds, and hold different values.

A recent survey of 1,600 women age fifty-plus, still available on the website www.womansage.com, found that baby-boomer women were (1) more comfortable with financial matters than their mothers had been, (2) talking about returning to school, (3) finding meaningful volunteer opportunities, and (4) interested in starting new businesses.[4]

Surprisingly similar to our one-to-one interviewees with women over sixty, the web-surveyed boomer women valued their independence and their control over their own lives, and they feared that they might lose these qualities should they be called upon to assume the care of dependent husbands, parents, or other relatives. These women viewed retirement as just another transition in their lives similar to previous transitions, and they believed that they had acquired many transition skills that they would apply again at another point in time. They were not ready to quit; they were beginning new ventures and cherishing this period as yet another opportunity to grow, contribute, and remain involved in the world. Boomer women often do not recognize that the generation of women that just precedes them have already plowed the ground that they are about to trod.

Another recent survey of 1,021 baby boomers, in this case ages fifty-five to sixty-four, resulted in findings that were both similar to those in the earlier Web survey and to the responses of our interviewees, age sixty to ninety-two and a half, in the study we conducted for this book.[5] What is striking is that although today's male and female baby boomers believe that they are on the leading edge of change when it comes to redefining the retirement years, the women of the Greatest Generation, their mothers, have already redefined these years and are currently living out alternative patterns in the third phase of their lives.

Survey results were reported publicly on June 28, 2007, at the Boomer Leading Change Forum, held at the University of Denver.[6] At that forum, there was a focus on the potential of harnessing the energies of the 78 million boomers, for civic engagement. A keynote presentation and book signing by Marc Freedman, author of *Encore: Finding Work That Matters in the Second Half of Life* and *Prime Time: How Baby Boomers Will Revolutionize Retirement and Transform America* and champion of public service in the retirement years, topped off the event.

The Colorado Boomers Leading Change study produced findings similar to other studies of boomers and revealed clearly that:

- Only 39 percent of the boomers plan to retire. More than half prefer or need to continue to work, at least part time or on a flexible schedule.
- Thirty-one percent of the men want a career change compared to 26 percent of the women.
- Thirty-one percent of the men want additional job training compared with 23 percent of the women.
- Sixty-five percent plan to take courses or engage in other learning experiences.
- Seventy-two percent plan to do volunteer work.[7]

Additional key findings of the Colorado study were that:

- Boomers want to remain engaged through work, service, and learning.
- Boomers anticipate significant changes in their work lives.
- Health care and retirement benefits, along with involvement with others and work that is meaningful, are the most important factors in their future lives.
- The top motivations for volunteering are passion for a cause, helping the community, feeling productive, and having meaning in their work.
- There is a disconnect between what service organizations report in how they utilize boomer volunteers and what boomers report about how they want to be utilized.
- There is a diversity of issues that capture boomers' interests.
- Sixty-five percent of the boomers report wanting to participate in lifelong learning.
- There is no one place where boomers will go to learn more about civic engagement if, in fact, they wish to know more about this topic.

Given that on their own, the women of the Greatest Generation have already been living out most of the boomers' stated lifestyle goals, the challenge now is to define how various institutions and businesses will be able to adapt to the needs of the baby boomers and how the experiences and talents of this large cohort will be utilized by our society. As one business leader put it, "As a nation, we need to take advantage of the energy and experience of our retirees in a way that will benefit both them and society as a whole."[8]

Also, the convergence of the values and lifestyles of women in the Greatest Generation and baby-boomer women presents a unique opportunity for intergenerational sharing and learning. The Greatest Generation women have valuable experiences to share and have the potential to play important roles in organizational change and mentor relationships as the baby boomers join them in their lengthening and active third stages of life. What a fine partnership that would be!

One way in which we have seen intergenerational mentoring taking place is when an older and more mature member of a community nonprofit board works collaboratively with a younger new professional who is hired as an executive director or staff person for that board. When these two parties are both women and when they like and respect each other, both learn a great deal and the organization gains from their partnership. The same is true in the workplace when a senior administrator extends herself to show the ropes to a new, lower-level staffer. In exchange, the younger employee may act as a technology mentor to the older woman, thereby balancing the shared nature of their relationship and enriching both parties. The organization's goals are furthered when this occurs, and women of two generations become more like colleagues than like employer and employee.

## The Voices of Our Interviewees

When we began discussions with our interviewees about this chapter, we said, "Chapter 8 is about attitudes: your attitudes about this time in your life and your views about how you are reinventing this period of your life. We also want to know what advice you would give the baby boomers who are just now entering their third thirds of life as they turn sixty."

As we analyzed our interviewees' attitudes about themselves and their lives at this stage, we found that a full 92 percent were positive in their self-descriptors. They described themselves as optimistic, energetic, accepting, pushing on, needing challenges, satisfied, grateful, and honest. One said modestly, after a lifetime of remarkable achievements, "I did my best." Another, who had led a fairly public life, said, "I took all the opportunities offered to me." And still another, who is known for her dry humor, said that she wanted her epitaph to read, "She lived until she died!"

Our interviewees reflected on how their life experiences may have changed their outlooks. In this process, they were equally positive. One very successful educator characterized herself as "always on the edge of doing something new." She said that this attitude was what has continued to motivate her at this stage of life. Many said that their attitudes now were "more expansive and inclusive," "less judgmental and more innovative," "more thoughtful and less self-centered." Most were eager to share their newer attitudes with younger women "to help them get nearer to experiences and feelings earlier and enjoy them longer." These women were not thinking about their lives ending, but rather about "pushing all I can into every day" so that their energies and new experiences could "rock a few more boats!"

This time of life was a period of serious introspection and self-criticism for some of our interviewees. Even though they were generally optimistic, they were not entirely sure that they were moving in the right direction. They were glad to have the opportunity to talk about their dilemmas and to discover that most of their contemporaries had many of the same concerns about living the rest of their lives as well as they had planned to. Several had family concerns about how to best pass on their values to their grandchildren, recognizing that some changes were bound to occur. They felt distressed about how work ethics, humanitarianism toward others, and the value of making lasting changes for the good of the next generation might be deteriorating.

Many of the women stated that they were positive and upbeat about their personal lives but were very distressed about the world. They worried about where we are heading as a nation and as a species. Had we had a longer time to talk, there probably would have been many more expressions of anxiety about the state of the world. As it was, some of the topics that did come up were wars, climate change, dependence on foreign oil, the lack of leadership by political figures, the state of education, conflicts about immigration, and health care policy. Yet in the brief discussions we did have, there were many ideas and suggestions about what might be done to ameliorate various basic problems that had had different faces in our interviewees' younger years.

One interviewee said, "I often think about Sandra Day O'Connor and how much she contributed to our society by serving on the Supreme Court. Her decision to retire seemed like such a personal one, and now she is in the public eye again. She's an interesting model for balancing public and private priorities."

Another mused, "I see so many atrocities, like in Rwanda, and I feel so helpless to do anything about them." One educator focused on the education system, "In spite of all that I and my colleagues accomplished, we barely moved the education system ahead. It's really a lifelong task to change an entire system, and even then, what we achieve seems so miniscule. And now, even an entire lifetime seems too short."

Because we tried to keep the focus of our interviews on personal matters not public affairs, we did not pursue these lines of discussion. But clearly such discussions are relevant and would be attractive as topics for TTT seminars for women much like our own thoughtful interviewees (see Appendix D).

## Messages to the Baby Boomers

In a conversation about this book with a young baby-boomer colleague, she was asked, "When you think about women over sixty, in the third third of their lives, what would you call them?" Without hesitation, she answered, "Wise!"

As we explored this idea further, we developed an acronym for WISE: W=well-informed, I=interesting, S=sophisticated, E=eloquent. That was the beginning of an interesting and creative discussion about the similarities and differences in the lives of contemporary women of different ages. The younger woman was a baby boomer in her forties, married, and had young children in elementary school. She held a very responsible position in her company, dealt with complex issues in her work, and supervised a number of employees. One of her special attributes was that she was always consciously looking for new colleagues who were somewhat her senior in age and from whom she could learn. It was clear that she valued the experience of older people, both men and women. She sought them out, hired them, and used their expertise to enrich her company. She thought of them as wise and had a strong enough ego to seek their advice and counsel. This is an example of how one sensitive and bright baby boomer enriched her own work life and served her company well by bringing in new talent from the Greatest Generation. This kind of intergenerational learning and work effort has the potential to greatly enrich and enhance the workplaces of the future. This one small vignette shows how, if developed consciously, older and younger workers and professionals could join hands in creating innovative, productive, and interesting intergenerational workplaces in the future. In this case, it was the younger woman who held the senior work position and invited the wise, more experienced older woman to participate in a project. It could also happen the other way around.

Similarly, whether wise or just experienced, our interviewees were not shy about offering their advice to the baby boomers and those even younger who will follow them into their sixties and beyond. Some of their unedited and anonymous remarks follow. Listen to the words of these especially thoughtful and insightful wise women over sixty. We urge our readers to read these words slowly and thoughtfully. When you are finished, read them again.

Some spoke about the philosophical side of life:

- "When fate deals you something, grieve, mourn, get over it, and move on."
- "It's time to leave a legacy. How will you be remembered?"
- "Look for simplicity and beauty in a world of chaos."
- "Uncover and use the gifts you've been given and take them into the world."
- "Look at your prejudices honestly and get rid of them."
- "You have more power than you think."
- "Don't take yourself so seriously."
- "Love life and cherish every minute."
- "Nature is our temple; love and duty our religion; the universe our God." (recalled from a cemetery tombstone)
- "Trust the unfolding. Now sit and enjoy. Turn to your spiritual self in your older years."
- "Create space for yourself. Ask, 'Who am I?'"
- "Take more risks. Move faster to clasp opportunities. Create something new."
- "Plumb resources and networks. Don't worry about a legacy."

Others spoke of friendship, relationships, marriage, and family:

- "Get younger friends."
- "Stay home with young children, then work."
- "Do your share in the friendship. When your husband dies, your friends are *it*."
- "Marrying is not right for everyone, but making a long relationship with another person is what helps you learn to be giving, forgiving, grateful, and peaceful. Give more to a relationship than you think you are getting."
- "Marry the right guy."
- "Enjoy your kids."

- "Establish your career before marriage; you'll have a better marriage."
- "Trust your own instincts. Choose friends you respect and who respect you."
- "Build a life that is self-sustaining and not dependent on a husband or anyone."
- "Let your kids lead their own lives."
- "Think about having children."

Then, there were bits of advice about work:

- "Be slow to retire...there are so many more opportunities for women now."
- "A career is never worth having unless you learn from it. Getting up and going to work means that you need to think about whether you are in the right place and make a change if you have to."

Others spoke about health:

- "Keep skiing, walking, and moving."
- "Stay fit and healthy. Keep your energy. Care for yourself. Plan a month of activity at a time."
- "Take care of your health—physical and mental."
- "Exercise and take vitamins."

Many spoke about goals and involvement:

- "Make new goals as soon as you achieve one. Don't waste time. Go out and *do it!*"
- "Institutions are not prepared for sixty-five and older."
- "Get involved in something you love and are interested in."
- "I did it *my* way. You do it *your way!*"

- "Keep your options open. Don't close any door. Keep on learning."
- "Have many interests."
- "Start each day with an agenda. Don't leave everything to chance. But when you have a new opportunity, show up, jump on it!"
- "Stay interested in the world around you. Be an active friend. Be active in politics or we will deserve the bad government we get."
- "Plan, plan, plan! And then be flexible!"

Others focused on giving back to the community:

- "Volunteer and give more."
- "Volunteer, share hope, and get new networks."
- "Extend yourself in the community. Don't be selfish."

Many gave overall advice about this third third of life:

- "Travel while you can."
- "Think about financial issues for later life. Life will become more difficult financially."
- "Don't think you're old at forty or fifty. I never thought I was old."
- "Keep busy. If you think you're old, you are."
- "Do financial planning to afford retirement."
- "Know when to leave an organization."
- "Our sixties is a nice time. There's a freedom and sense of time for reflection."
- "Things come together at this time of life…many problems are not there anymore. There's a relief, a freedom. Look over your achievements."
- "Do a journal. Take notes. Stay active. Manage your own money. Be kind to everyone."

- "Don't cut yourself off from experience. Don't sweat the small stuff. Enjoy friendships, travel, keep on learning. Do things that keep you young. Be open to new ideas."
- "Use your time before sixty to reflect on what you really want to do."
- "Every age has its issues. We need a group for discussion, a new organization for women in their sixties and seventies. Maybe we should call it the Third Trimester Women's Association."
- "This time of our lives is a continuum of prior years. You can't see immediately the results of relationships, work, and family. The last chapter is not yet written...and we don't know how it's going to turn out."
- "We have been the definers of new women's roles and are still on the cutting edge of new women's roles. Go for it! Keep finding something really interesting."
- "Mend dissonances in the family. Stay close to younger people."
- "Find interests outside the home. Don't atrophy. Travel, meet new people, go to new places. Read!"
- "Develop as many interests as possible."
- "Appreciate the decade you are in."
- "Balance society's expectations and your own."
- "Exhale: take a day at a time."
- "Compartmentalize: keep time for yourself."
- "Find good people: men and women."
- "Develop your own interests early."
- "Dreams are worth pursuing at any age."
- "Plan for the third-third transition. Do a financial plan. Do satisfying work after sixty-five."
- "Our kids are grown; it's a glorious time; celebrate! This is a good time of life; it's fulfilling. We are lucky."

We all know the common phrase "Those who cannot learn from history are doomed to repeat it."[9] The advice given above by the women of the Greatest Generation to the baby-boomer women is valuable, worth contemplating and considering seriously. Take it to heart.

## Woman to Woman

For many years, we have thought that women prosper in intergenerational environments. However, such environments are still exceedingly rare. When extended families lived near one another, family gatherings and holidays provided for intergenerational communication and learning. Now that most families are spread out into different parts of the country and the world, such exchanges are rare, if they exist at all. As a response to this phenomenon, many women today have created extended families of friends and neighbors who behave like blood relatives did in the past: sharing holiday dinners, organizing babysitting cooperatives, scheduling play dates for children of similar ages, meeting regularly for book groups or other shared hobbies, cooking and having potluck suppers, and finding ways to be part of a family, whether related by blood or not. Still, these groups may not be very diverse in terms of including different generations.

One of the wonderful outcomes of the women's movement is that it provided spaces and events that put diverse women in touch with one another. Friendships were forged across the boundaries of age, income, and ethnicity, often in consciousness-raising groups. Women formed many new formal organizations, both professional societies and networking groups. Sometimes, within corporations and other workplaces, women organized internal women's organizations. We all learned a great deal about both ourselves and each other from those experiences. We also performed a wide variety of volunteer tasks and projects, often directed at younger members of that particular group, such as creating scholarships, mentor programs, career orientations, and job fairs. Now, more than forty years later, those of us in our third thirds have learned from life's experiences and lessons just at the time when the baby boomers are entering this new stage of their lives and new opportunities for woman-to-woman sharing are beginning to appear. New Internet-based networks are connecting more people than ever. The time is now ripe to create purposeful intergenerational, Web-based sites that encourage the connection between baby-boomer women and women of the Greatest Generation. Maybe your next mentor relationship or friendship lies just under the click of your finger. Who knows?

# CHAPTER 9

# From a Room of Our Own
# to a Time of Our Own

**A woman must have money and a room of her own.**
—Virginia Woolf, *A Room of Her Own*, 1929

## A Little Review

We began this book somewhat autobiographically in the hopes that our readers would identify with our personal, professional, and community experiences. We continued by introducing a concept that has guided the development of this book: the third third of life. We then explained the life cycle in developmental terms and laid a conceptual foundation, drawing on the work of various theoreticians, researchers, and writers. We recalled that turning sixty was truly a marker event in which many new and perplexing questions came into focus. This third third of life presents most of us with important and new challenges and decisions. In many ways, this final phase is going to be a qualitatively different time of our lives.

We then introduced our forty interviewees, women between the ages of sixty and ninety-two and a half. Those forty women, in addition to the participants in our fourteen small groups, framed the issues in this book and gave us insight into the changes that were taking place in our society among women in their third third of life. In those one-to-one discussions we were able to confirm our basic hypothesis, that women over sixty are experiencing a new sense of freedom and are truly living in a time of their own.

In our second chapter, we began to explore the very concept of retirement and how our interviewees related to the idea of reinvention, or redefinition, of their lives after sixty. Most of their thinking revolved around the freedom they were experiencing because: (1) their children had grown into adulthood and were on their own and (2) they had completed their midlife career goals, thereby freeing them up for using their time and resources in ways they themselves chose. Rather than dreading their aging years, our interviewees were rejoicing in the new opportunities these years offered. And although they may not have used such words as *reinvention* or *redefinition*, they were embarking on new paths and adventures for which they had no role models, given that their mothers' lives had been very different from their own. For today's women over sixty, the themes of reinvention, redefinition, renewal, and revival are apropos. These women are the first generation in history to have the good health, experience, and opportunity of starting anew during the third third of their lives. This is a rare and remarkable situation.

Reinvention leads to new roles and responsibilities. The persistent question "What am I going to be when I grow up?" reappears just as the three identity-seeking questions of life—Who am I? To what groups do I belong? How do I function?—may return and demand answers once again.

Responsibilities for others, especially spouses in ill health, remain part of our third-third lives. Grandchildren give us great pleasure and opportunities to participate in yet another generation's development. Yet, some of our parents still remain, lending reality to the term *sandwich generation*, meaning a generation that cares for both its young and its elders at the same time and is often caught between these compelling demands. In our third third of life, we give more time to relationships and friendships. Spirituality becomes important to some. Our diverse roles could be summarized as caretaker, interdependent, dependent, or independent. Most of us are filling a mixture of these roles in our later years, and there are significant changes in these roles as health and other dimensions of our lives and our loved ones' lives continue to change.

Work has always been a central feature of women's lives, be it domestic, professional, or commercial. Our mothers' generation often had to choose between the work of raising a family and work outside the home. Our generation found ways to do both. The women's movement reframed our family and work balance, and the efforts we made to achieve success in both arenas have become the innovative and creative habits that we are now using in the third third of our lives. Our interviewees clearly demonstrated that the women of our generation focused on work for many reasons: to generate income, for intellectual stimulation, for collegial relationships, and for giving purpose and meaning to their lives. For the most part, no matter what the level of sophistication of their jobs, these women enjoyed their work and derived much satisfaction from it. As a result, many continue to work, even well into their eighties, and they are setting the pace for the baby-boomer generation relative to changing the concept of retirement. These women are redefining what retirement now means: full-time work, part-time work, flexible schedules, shared jobs, phased retirement, and work from home, as well as traditional retirement. Even though institutions and businesses have been slow to respond to these changes, the Greatest Generation women are leading the way toward reinventing new work patterns in the third third of life.

Rather than view this period of life as the end of work, these women have created a free and creative transitional time when the challenge is to continue to work at activities that are meaningful and purposeful, be they paid or volunteer activities. As in all transitions, there are phases of discontent and confusion before a new equilibrium and sense of coherence are achieved. Once having established that new equilibrium, these Greatest Generation women begin to reveal what the new sixty looks like, and they are laying the groundwork for the 78 million baby boomers on how to remain not only active, but also productive.

Many in this generation of women have been the most productive in their volunteer lives. They served their communities throughout World War II, the Korean War, and Vietnam. They volunteered during the civil rights movement, the women's movement, the peace movement, and the environmental movement. They are master organizers and are politically aware. Volunteerism has been a central part of their behavior, values, and lifestyles, and their service is continuing in the third third of their lives.

According to *Time* magazine, in 2006 61.2 million Americans volunteered 8.1 billion hours.[1] A plan for universal national service is currently being proposed.[2] As public service becomes an even more important element in our society, women over sixty can and will play leading roles in this new twenty-first-century volunteer movement. Public service and volunteerism are threads that are woven into the very fabric of these women's lives. Among our Greatest Generation interviewees were ex–Peace Corps volunteers, administrators of non-profits that rely solely or heavily on volunteers, and women who had founded various kinds of community organizations. There is a huge potential to tap into the experience of this large pool of mature women. If efforts were made to value and recruit these women, our nation and communities would be the winners. At the same time, a new wave of public service and volunteerism could add meaning and a renewed sense of purpose to many women's third-third years.

We have learned that money is not a trivial element of our older years. In fact, it is a central variable that frames and often determines the quality of life after sixty. Because many women have not had a great deal of experience with money management, they sometimes lack confidence in their ability to preserve and grow their financial resources. But no matter if a woman is married, single, divorced, or widowed, it is likely that she will need to be responsible for the financial aspects of her life at some point. Women frequently outlive their spouses and must seek financial advice or make decisions on their own. Since women still earn considerably less than men, even for similar jobs, Social Security and other retirement programs will net them less. For some of our interviewees, that negative circumstance was offset by inheritance funds, annuity or insurance benefits, or the communal funds of a religious community to which they belonged. In some cases, they were living quite comfortably on these sources of income. The women who were facing the most challenging situations relative to money were divorcees and widows whose earnings were relatively modest and those who had lifelong dependents with health problems that were draining their finances. Those were the women who most needed to plan early for their lengthening nonworking retirements and who would be able to profit from having professional financial expertise to assist them. This remains an unmet need, as not all women have access to financial experts.

Our country's economic climate continues to change. Since the future economy remains unknown and the effects of globalization are unpredictable, women are required to be more alert to possible changes that could materially and negatively affect their financial health. As we talked with our interviewees and read background materials, it became clear that women are aware of this need and are willing to share information and ideas, even when they are informal and experiential. But even if women admit their readiness to share financial insights with one another, we do not have well-honed habits of discussing financial matters with each other or a women's culture that supports the trading of tips on ways to make money.

Women who are now working have opportunities to seek financial help from their employers' resources. For others, there are many retirement planning seminars put on by financial and educational institutions, self-help pamphlets and books in stores and libraries, and a number of financial advisors who offer one-to-one consultation with the goal of investing and managing the client's financial resources. For several of our interviewees, younger family members have been excellent tutors and have been supportive in dealing with money matters as women find themselves needing up-to-date advice. It is important for women who have access to these kinds of resources to remain aware and concerned about their less financially sophisticated female compatriots, as well as those who will soon enter this age group. Good planning is the best method of ensuring financial security in the future.

Regardless of their financial circumstances, all the women we interviewed were concerned about the possibility of a catastrophic illness or long-term health needs that required large expenditures of funds. They all hoped they had covered themselves for the future. But, in truth, one does not really know until the time comes. Bottom line: It's better to have money than not, and young women really need to take responsibility for their own third-third financial security—the sooner the better.

In our chapter on health, we tried to accomplish two things: (1) discuss women's health in general and (2) give information on conditions that are common to women in our older years, with examples specific to our interviewees. The most fundamental concept we tried to project is that *old* and *sick* are not synonymous. Just because we are getting older does not necessarily mean that we are getting sicker. It is also clear that older people are not focused on dying: they are focused on living!

However, there are many normal changes in our bodies as we age, and we do have to adapt to those. But while our bodies may lose some of their youthful characteristics, odds are good that our minds will remain intact, our intelligence will be sharp, and our wisdom about life will surely increase. Latent talents may reappear, and we may have more time to pursue our interests. The goal is "positive aging," and the wise management of common health issues is critical to our attitudes as well as to our actual health. We were pleased to find that a third of our interviewees did not have any significant health problems, proving once again that to age does not mean to be sick. We are not only living longer, we are living healthier.

In our brief summaries of common health problems, we included arthritis, chronic pain, cardiovascular disease, stroke and neurological disease, memory loss, oral health, gastrointestinal problems, diabetes, osteoporosis, orthopedic problems, and cancer. These mostly chronic conditions require vigilance and management. Additionally, since medications require management and can be such a great cost issue in our aging years, a few tips about drugs are included.

With our interviewees, we investigated a number of other health-related concerns: the health of families and friends, aging parents, plans in the event of severe health problems, health insurance, and long-term care insurance. We stressed the importance of the psychological and attitudinal aspects of aging, shared research about "successful aging" and "positive aging," and suggested strategies for coping with the changes that occur in this Third-Third Transition.

It has been inspiring for us to learn about people around the world who are over one hundred years of age and have adopted attitudes and activities that have kept them alive and well. Similarly, our own interviewees are essentially well, even as many have surmounted serious health issues and diseases. Now that they have recovered from various illnesses, they remain active, positive, productive, and optimistic. It has become almost a cliché to say it, but the marvels of modern medicine and our prosperous lifestyles have extended our lives and made our third-third years healthier and more livable than ever before. Most women will now live into their eighties, and many of us will be around into our nineties. These trends indicate that our years after sixty may extend beyond one-third of our lives. In fact, centenarians are one of the fastest growing segments of our population.

One cannot stay retired at leisure for more than thirty years and remain interesting and interested in life. It is imperative that we include work, volunteerism, travel, community service, physical and mental activities, creativity, relationships, and family involvement in our third-third years, in addition to leisure activities. How many of us could have imagined that we would be so healthy in our years over sixty? What a pleasure it is to have a bonus time in our lives during which we can make use of our accumulated experience and wisdom and take full advantage of all that our remarkable world has to offer!

As we concluded our interviews, we wanted to know more about what real losses and regrets women over sixty might report. The most frequent losses were of loved ones through death, especially of parents, partners, children, and friends. The loss of parents thrusts us into the role of "the older generation," sometimes in premature and untimely ways. The loss of a partner, through death or divorce, changes our own lives the most. We grieve the loss of children for the rest of our lives. The loss of friends is both the most common and one of the saddest.

Regret is a special kind of loss. It is a loss of something that was anticipated but did not happen. Although some of our interviewees expressed no regrets, an equal number regretted not having done certain things related to people. We seem to regret very deeply incomplete

191

or unsatisfactory relationships. But most of our interviewees' regrets related to their careers. They regretted career paths not chosen, not starting careers earlier, not being ambitious enough in their career choices. However, all in all, they did not regret the careers they chose, they simply thought they could have gone further in their work than they actually did. Perhaps that sentiment is attributable to the fact that today's third-third women were career pioneers, and being the first generation of contemporary working women to juggle families, education, and careers outside the home, they simply did not have the time nor had our society advanced enough for all doors to be open to them.

Our interviewees' gains were many. First among them were grandchildren. Nothing gave these women more pleasure than having and enjoying their grandchildren. But the most significant gain of this time of life was clearly freedom. More than anything else, when we reach sixty and beyond, we gain a new kind of freedom: the freedom to be oneself, to make one's own decisions, to give back to society, and to pursue our day without the constraints of family or job responsibilities. This is a special time for inner development, a time to think and to consider, a time to remember and to savor, a time to be grateful for every day.

## The Future

At this point, we would like to venture into the unknown, gaze into our crystal ball, and consider what lies ahead in the twenty-first century for women over sixty.

First, as our life spans lengthen and our health continues to improve, the years beyond sixty might be redefined into two phases: phase I, from age sixty to age eighty, and phase II, from age eighty to age one hundred and beyond. In the future, these two phases of our lives may possibly stretch over forty or more years rather than thirty.

Second, as a result, we may once again be in a process of reinvention and redefinition. The sixty- to eighty-year-olds could look and feel relatively young, more like midlifers than like the elderly. Those over eighty could remain active and busy until their health causes them to slow down. That may not be until their mid-nineties or later.

These years could be a wonderful time of redefining roles, especially in intergenerational activities with younger generations of women and girls, with all of us learning and benefiting. What fun!

Third, this lengthening vigor could make it possible for women to continue to multitask and play multiple roles of great-grandmother, grandmother, mother, and spouse simultaneously, for many years. Families may commonly contain not only three, but four or five living generations. Our long-term friends may become even more like family, and holiday celebrations may expand in size and diversity. Our relationships are likely to become richer, since we will have more time to nurture them. Golden wedding anniversaries could become commonplace, and special marriage advisors might begin to deal with the issues of marriage in our mature years. As we grow older, women will have to be aware of the aging men in their lives and look for ways to mutually enjoy the changes that occur for them as they struggle with similar new roles, new ideas, and new needs. Physical dependency, psychological codependency, dual nursing home arrangements, and separate spousal living quarters could need to be explored and might become common.

Fourth, some of the biggest changes may take place in the world of work. More people may want and need to work well into their seventies and even during their eighties. In fact, the whole concept of retirement will likely undergo radical change. Fewer people will be able to afford to retire in the traditional sense, that is, to not work at all. Institutions, businesses, and governments will likely create new policies that will not only permit but encourage people to remain on the job for as long as they wish and are able to perform their duties. Perhaps there will be trade-offs between employers and Social Security: more individuals may be able to collect Social Security while continuing to work and earn an income. At the same time, they may continue to pay taxes that, in turn, will help to support the Social Security system. Or, employers might retain older workers who will cut back on their hours and forgo Social Security for additional years but not have FICA and other deductions made from their paychecks, so that their take-home pay remains adequate while they gain additional nonworking flexible time.

Globalization offers opportunities for creative ideas regarding work. Once-retired persons could help businesses by traveling to evaluate distant new prospects, thus freeing younger workers with growing families to remain closer to home. Learning new languages is key to doing business in the global marketplace and could appeal to older people looking for intellectual stimulation and novel challenges that are socially and economically useful.

The key point here is that a new customized contract could be forged between the elderly individual, the employer, and government that would result in slowing the growth of Social Security payments, increasing work flexibility, retaining experience in the workplace, increasing government tax receipts, and freeing up more time for volunteerism and public service.

Marc Freedman has made extensive suggestions in this arena in *Encore: Finding Work That Matters in the Second Half of Life*. Freedman envisions people ending their first career early and creating a second "encore career" in public-service arenas while government develops a second New Deal, this time rebalancing the financial aspects of working and retirement as well as time use. His organization, Civic Ventures, has played a leading role in both conceptualizing and implementing a wide variety of projects that address social needs by redefining purposeful paid work, as well as nonpaid volunteer public service, in our older years.[3]

We have reached a time in history when we have an educated, experienced, and healthy workforce that is not interested in spending thirty or forty years in leisure retirement activities. Further, many of the women of this and future generations who returned to the workforce after their children were grown and on their own, perhaps in their mid-forties, have barely gotten started at work at age sixty or sixty-five; they are hardly ready to retire.

Fifth, in the future, women will be more open and knowledgeable about money and will be more likely to have done financial planning, earned their own incomes, become investors, and provided for their own financial security. Enlightened women's organizations, clubs, and schools currently provide some of these services as they recognize that women need to start saving money early so they are prepared to support themselves later in life. We are hopeful that as women view their increasing financial independence as essential, they will have resource networks and employers that will be able to provide financial planning services to them. We also expect that as women's earning power increases as professional and executive positions become ever more available to them, they will aspire to conserving their assets for their older, nonworking years.

Sixth, the changes in our health, health care, and the management of health will rival in scope the changes in work and will create an entirely new set of circumstances in our lives from age sixty to one hundred and beyond. Strides in bioscience are likely to ameliorate many diseases and cure others. More preventive health measures are now included in the entire concept of health care and health insurance as the employers and those in industry—even health care—learn the old adage "An ounce of prevention is worth a pound of cure." Medical and pharmaceutical advances will continue, allowing people to replace most joints and organs, trace their genetic material for therapeutic purposes, and receive medications to treat both chronic and acute illnesses. When arthritis no longer keeps people from hiking and biking, they will continue to do those activities. When breast cancer no longer requires radical mastectomies and extensive chemotherapy, women will be freed from their fears of this mysterious and overwhelming disease. Both women and men can look forward to less morbidity from heart disease as newer biomechanical "heart parts" give them better quality of life and preventive lifestyle measures gain further support by individuals and the health system. As we gain more knowledge of and empathy for chronic illnesses in older persons and increase our awareness of the health burden of conditions such as diabetes, high blood pressure, obesity, and lung disease among younger generations, overall health in later life can be improved. Research and practice continue to add knowledge in the health field. As more people consider themselves to be the main partner with health professionals in the pursuit of good health and assume more personal responsibility for caring for themselves and their families, we may get a handle on how to stop the burgeoning costs related to health care.

Women continue to be the main health monitors of the family's health. There is no sign that this role will diminish among future generations of women. It provides more opportunities for us to collaborate intergenerationally and find better answers to daily health dilemmas.

Health care is already changing more dramatically than has been documented for the public. The mix of primary care and specialty physicians has shifted in favor of specialists, and many older patients who are on Medicare and Medicaid cannot find a primary care physician who will accept them. The health care system depends on referral from primary care physicians and nurse practitioners to specialists. The payment system depends on this line of reference as well. So if someone knows they need a dermatologist, they may not be able to refer themselves and still get it paid for. This keeps the access to needed care well guarded. Further, if they have a preexisting medical condition, they may not be able to find an insurance company that will cover them at all. If the first step is accomplished, they may find the maze of paperwork to get referred to the best person to deal with their particular problem daunting. This is an intolerable set of circumstances that will have to be addressed if there is to be any way for older people to receive medical care that is appropriate, and in many cases, at all.

If the management of health care continues to remain in the hands of the private sector, a serious resolution of our current dilemmas must be found. Health care policies must be restructured by and for the providers, the facilities, the pharmaceutical industry, the insurance industry, the government, the employers, and most important of all, the patients. This collaborative effort will be long and difficult. But as more and more Americans face the health changes brought on by aging, it is imperative that we restructure our health care system to care for them.

Seventh, losses and regrets will continue. Life is like that. We will still lose parents, children, relatives, and friends to untimely diseases and accidents. Losses in our marriages, our workplaces, and our communities will continue to disappoint us as well. So we should become more adept at seeking counseling and support groups to ameliorate these conditions. However, as women now have more educational and career opportunities, as well as simultaneous opportunities for family-building in their early adulthoods, they may have fewer regrets about their careers and education in the future, for the antidote to regret is opportunity. As more women assume leadership positions in the private and public sectors, it is increasingly likely that opportunities for women will widen.

The gains enumerated by our Greatest Generation women will be multiplied many times over by those who follow them. The contemporary women's movement is less than fifty years old, and already there have been major changes in the lives of American women. In another fifty years, when our granddaughters and great-granddaughters are in the third third of their lives, women will have opportunities for communal living, global travel, work and careers of their own definition, more effective family-work balances, increased lifelong learning opportunities, and caring communities within which to live. Women are likely to have more opportunities for a wider variety of lifestyles wherein diversity is both increased and accepted. Women will lead many new, less linear ways of life: more single women will give birth to and adopt children, women will live together in small groups as well as couples, and alternating work with travel and leisure transitions over many years will become more commonplace. There is no turning back from the gains that women have made, and there is a strong likelihood that those gains will steadily but surely increase in both number and substance.

Some of the most important gains to which we aspire are beyond our country's borders. It is critical that we as a nation begin to take a leadership position in creating a "new world order" ensuring that peace will prevail and that women in the underdeveloped parts of the world have opportunities for education, family planning, and income-producing work. Improvements in access to health care for women and children are sorely needed. Women must claim their human rights and insist that they become equal partners in building their societies. And women must not allow another generation to go to war. This is the great unfinished work of our time.

Our eighth glimpse into the future reveals that the baby boomers, our own sons and daughters, can learn the lessons of the twentieth century and apply them to the twenty-first. Perhaps they will seek more ideas and advice from the Greatest Generation women in their lives: their mothers, aunts, and teachers. Perhaps they will organize intergenerational discussions, both virtually and in person, to provide arenas for the regular exchange of ideas. Perhaps they will create Third-Third Transition groups, websites, conferences, publications, films, and media specials about life from sixty to one hundred, thereby examining many emerging issues and creating resources for us all.

All of us look to the generation prior to our own for experience and wisdom. We also look to the next generation for hope and a vision for the future. Now that multiple generations are living at the same time, we have an important opportunity to know and learn from one another. We also have an opportunity to celebrate the gains that twentieth-century women have made and the contributions they have given society. It would be a shame for us waste this rare moment in history.

For now is truly a time of our own.

# About Chapter 10

You've probably noticed that there is no Chapter 10 in this book. That chapter is not yet written. We left this space for you and invite you to write the last chapter yourself. You may address the topics that we included in this book:

- The Third Third of Life
- The Concept of Reinvention
- Changing Roles, Responsibilities, and Relationships
- Women and Work
- Women and Money
- Women and Health
- Losses, Regrets, and Gains
- From Generation to Generation
- From a Room of Our Own to a Time of Our Own

Or, you may choose those topics of most importance to you as you redefine and reinvent your own unique third third of life. After all, this is the last chapter for all of us.

The following blank pages are yours to use as you wish. We hope that you make this last chapter of your life truly a time of your very own.

Best Wishes,
Elinor Miller Greenberg
and Fay Wadsworth Whitney

# Life Is a Journey

Birth is a beginning and death a destination;
But life is a journey.
A going, a growing from stage to stage:
From childhood to maturity and youth to old age.
From innocence to awareness and ignorance to knowing;
From foolishness to discretion and then perhaps, to wisdom.
From weakness to strength or strength to weakness and often
    back again.
From health to sickness and back we pray, to health again.
From offense to forgiveness, from loneliness to love,
From joy to gratitude, from pain to compassion.
From grief to understanding, from fear to faith;
From defeat to defeat to defeat, until, looking backward or ahead:
We see that victory lies not at some high place along the way,
But in having made the journey, stage by stage, a sacred pilgrimage.
Birth is a beginning and death a destination;
But life is a journey, a sacred pilgrimage,
Made stage by stage...To life everlasting.

—Rabbi Alvin I. Fine

A book is a wondrous thing. Even though we now have many electronic devices with which to communicate, there is something very personal and special about a book. We are very proud to have had the opportunity to produce this book and to share it with you. Many people have been part of the journey of creating this book. We'd like to thank them and express our sincere appreciation for their generosity.

First, we thank our interviewees and other women with whom we conferred, and without whom we could not have written this book. They told us about their deepest fears and joys, shared with us their hopes and dreams, and gave us their precious time and thoughtful ideas without reservation. To these remarkable women between the ages of sixty and ninety-two, we say "thank you" from the bottom of our hearts: Kathy Abraham, Alice Abrams, Hazel Brown, Saundra Clayton, Eulalia Conde, Jean Carol Crump, Sandra Dallas, Rose DeMaeo, Marion P. Downs, Hannah Evans, Virginia (Ginny) Fraser, Joan Griffin, Margaret (Meg) S. Hansson, Jean C. Jones, Bernie Kern, Maybelle Krekeler, June Kyle, Dottie Lamm, Bernice (Bernie) Lane, Sally Lloyd, Alice Loughrey, Carolyn Lynch, Patricia Jean (PJ) Manion, Betty Marler (deceased), Emily McCall, Susan (Susie) McKay, Joan Mills, Agnes Milstead, Patricia (Pat) Murrell, Virginia (Ginny) S. Newton, Adele Phelan, Judy Powell, Patricia Barela Rivera, Lynne Simpson, Barbara Smith, Susan Stark, Janice (Jan) Steinhauser, Carol Sullivan, Deborah Trephan, Karolyn VanDeveer, Jane Vennard, Merrily Wallach, and Sharon Weinberg.

Next, we wish to express our appreciation to the members of the Health Matters small groups that met between 2002 and 2007 for their insights into the health concerns and ideas that contributed mainly to the health chapter, but to others as well. They were candid and willing to share from the start. For the men who also attended and added greatly to this group, we appreciated a glimpse into what men over sixty have done with issues they face in their lives. They, too, resemble the strength and vitality of our interviewees and group participants who were women.

Some of the professional researchers, many of whom have been our personal colleagues and friends, upon whose work ours is built and to whom we owe an enormous debt are Bill Bergquist, Bill Charland, Art Chickering, Larry Daloz, Erik Erikson, Lois Evans, Claire Fagan, Arthur Fine, Betty Friedan, Morris Keeton, Alan Klaum, David Kolb, Daniel Levinson, Barbara Love, Mathey Mezey, William G. Perry Jr., Gail Sheehy, Neville Strumpf, Jill Tarule, Sheila Tobias, and Rita Weathersby. Their lifelong work and perspectives have illuminated the phases, stages, and styles of the human life cycle and form the theoretical and practical basis for our own work and for this book.

And this book could not have been completed without the enthusiasm and encouragement of our publisher, Fulcrum Publishing, of Golden, Colorado, and their marvelous and talented staff: Bob Baron, Charlotte Baron, Faith Marcovecchio, and Erin Palmiter.

Finally, we wish to acknowledge that were it not for our work together in the Mountain and Plains Partnership (MAPP) Project, a component of the National Partnerships for Training Project, funded by the Robert Wood Johnson Foundation between 1995 and 2002, we might never have met and this book might never have been born. This shows that even in the third third of our lives, unanticipated new things occur that bring new opportunities for growth and creativity. Life is full of wondrous surprises, interesting and open friendships and relationships, and books...which, indeed, are wondrous things.

With deep appreciation,
Elinor Miller Greenberg
and Fay Wadsworth Whitney

# Interview Guide

## Introduction

This Interview Guide was designed for this book. The Guide was intended to assist in our interviews with forty women over sixty. These one-to-one interviews were conducted mostly in person; a few were done over the telephone. Each interview lasted approximately two hours. Detailed notes were taken during the interviews. This commonly used qualitative research methodology made extensive use of "probes" to encourage our interviewees to expand on their ideas and responses. We first told our interviewees about this book and thanked them for being willing to be interviewed. The interview questions below follow the order of the book's chapters.

<u>Chapter 1</u> – Developing the idea of the **third-third** or **third trimester of life**.

- When you hear me describe this time of your life as the "third-third/third trimester of life," what does it make you think of?
- How would you broadly characterize this time of your life after sixty and how would you label it?
- Probe question could be: Are there specific characteristics of this age that you think most women could agree on? What are they?

<u>Chapter 2</u> – Developing the idea of **reinvention**, or a substitute concept such as **redefinition**, for how women feel their older years may differ or be the same as the previous generations of the same age.

- Thinking about yourself and your peers in relation to women in your mother's generation, what might be similarities or differences between the two generations?
- What model for women over sixty would you use to describe this period of life in today's world?
- Probe question could be: Is it, perhaps, a time of reinventing oneself? Of deepening ties? Of creating a new or reviving an earlier latent talent?

**Chapter 3** – Finding **new roles and new relationships/religion** at this time of life and how these roles are strengthened and played out in present society. The focus is on relationships with spouses, friends, males, grandchildren, aunts, sisters, parents, and so on at a new time in life. Issues of spirituality and religion are also explored.

- Because women are veteran multitaskers, both by training and disposition, what do you see are the multiple roles at your present age?
- Are the roles you now have different than before? How and why do you think so?
- How do you build networks or use networks already available to you now?
- Does religion play a particular role in your life at this time? Say something about both organized religion and spirituality.
- Probe questions could be: Do you see your role as daughter, wife, community participant, and so on differently than you might have several years ago? What new roles have become most important now?

**Chapter 4** – The concepts of **work and volunteering** and how they have affected women earlier in life and now.

- We have chosen to focus on working women because of the tremendous changes that have come about due to of both the number of women entering the workforce and their positions now, as opposed to when we were younger. Tell me what you see as your work trajectory throughout your life.

- What does it now mean to be aging with retirement as an option?
- What difficulties or opportunities are present because of your work?
- Volunteering has often played a role in women's activities. Are you volunteering now? Where? Compare your volunteering now to past years.
- Probe questions could be: Tell me more about your work and your retirement plans. Are you looking forward to retirement, or do you expect to continue working as long as you can?

**Chapter 5** – Looking for **money** questions and those of **wealth/poverty.** What are the financial issues that these women have that concern them? What are the options they have chosen so far that they see as successful ways to cope with roles and status changes in this phase of life?

- There are probably many questions you have about how you should deal with changing economic issues in your life now. What are some of them?
- What preplanning and other successful strategies have you found to deal with these financial issues?
- Probe question might be: If this area of your life is worrisome to you, who do you have to help you deal with it?

**Chapter 6** – Investigating **health** issues. We tried to elicit three categories, at least, of things related to health issues: (1) What health issues do you have? (2) What family/friends have health issues that now affect you? and (3) How do you expect to solve the issues of caregiving and care-receiving?

- As you have grown older, how healthy do you feel in relation to others in your age group? What are some health problems you deal with and how do you handle them?
- Are your friends and family well, or do you have responsibilities related to their health? How are you handling these issues?
- What plans have you made for your own living arrangements as you are aging? What questions are vexing in relation to this issue?
- Probe questions might be: Do you consider yourself generally healthy and active? Is your or your family's health becoming a barrier to your continued activities?

**Chapter 7** – Developing the ideas of **losses, regrets, and gains** in this stage of life.

- For some people, growing older seems full of losses and changes that affect their lives negatively. For others, new opportunities seem to arise from the new circumstances losses and changes can cause, and they see gains in this time of life. Tell me about your ideas in relation to this.
- Do you have any regrets? Anything you did not do that you think you should have done? Anything you did that you are sorry for?
- What are the most significant gains in your life at this time? What are some of the best things happening in your life now?
- Probe question might be: Can you give me an example of some situations that describe the losses, regrets, and gains in your life?

**Chapter 8** – The culmination of the interview, especially about **"new attitudes."** This is our major advice chapter for reinvention after age sixty.

- What do you think about the idea of reinvention in this phase of your life?
- What advice would you give younger women, the baby boomers and others who are even younger, who will enter this phase in the future?
- Probe question might be: Is there anything else you'd like to say that we may have missed?

**Chapter 9** – This chapter on the **future** was developed after the interviews were completed and as a result of writing and reviewing the findings of the interviews and our other research.

**Afterword: Chapter 10** – The idea of having the reader follow the same sequence of thought as we did in writing this book was developed as we completed the manuscript and began to consider ways in which the book might be used.

# Health Matters Topics

The Health Matters group came into being in 2002, when Fay Whitney saw a need for neighbors in her condominium to have better access to up-to-date information about common health problems. An informal group was gathered each week for four months each year. All residents were invited, and both women and men made up the participant group of twelve to twenty-five people in attendance. Most were women, but slowly more men joined the group as well. Guests attended when visiting their family and friends in the condominium. The group was composed largely of those over sixty. Participation was voluntary. The hour-long meetings took the form of a short presentation by the facilitator about the chosen topic followed by discussion and questions among participants. Topics included:

1. Neuropathies – Tingles, Pains, and Numbness
2. Eye Problems – Coping With What You See or Don't See
3. Keeping You and Your Heart Ticking – New Thoughts
4. Breathing – In and Out, or Not: Pulmonary Problems
5. The Truth about Forgetting and Aging – What's Up!
6. The Slippery Slope – You and Your Immune System
7. The Value and Down Side of Stress in Your Life
8. Mental Health Is Not the Same as Mental Disease
9. Insurance and the Health Care System for You
10. Retirement, Retreading, Rethinking, Reinvention?
11. And So to Sleep – Getting the Best Rest
12. Cholesterol, Lipids, Drugs, and You
13. "Oh Sugar"! Diabetes Control for Type 2s
14. Stress: The Good, the Bad, and the Ugly
15. Marketing Youth: Antiaging Potions
16. Strategies for Successful, Positive Aging

# Reliable Health Resources on the Web

This list was designed to provide a starting place for Web-based information on some health-related topics you might want to pursue further. It is certainly not an exhaustive list. Many of these resources are located on National Institutes of Health (NIH) websites, because the NIH has reliable information and pathways to other reliable sources on the Internet. When seeking health advice on the Web, always use www.nih.gov to look for the topic you are interested in. Your public library can also help you find Internet resources. If you would like other ways to contact organizations, addresses and phone numbers are often provided on the websites.

Professional organizations are also good sources of reliable websites and avenues to the kinds of information you are seeking. The Yellow Pages of state and local telephone books have listings for many professional associations, as do local health providers. Use caution in doing your search for information and trust your own evaluations of the information provided. If it looks too good to be true, it probably is. Wishing you good health and good luck!

## General Aging
• National Institute on Aging – National Institutes of Health (research, information, national gateway to aging): www.nia.nih.gov
• Gerontological Society of America: www.geron.org

## Arthritis
• www.rheumatology.org
• www.arthritis.org

## Brain/Memory Improvement
• Brain aerobics and puzzles: www.happyneuron.com

## Diabetes

- Centers for Disease Control and Prevention 2005 National Diabetes Fact Sheet: General Information and National Estimates on Diabetes in the United States: www.cdc.gov/diabetes/pubs/pdf/ndfs_2005.pdf
- American Diabetes Association: www.diabetes.niddk.nih.gov
- National Diabetes Information Clearinghouse: http://diabetes.niddk.nih.gov/resources/organizations.htm

## Drug Information

- National Institute of Allergy and Infectious Diseases (NIAID), National Institute of Health Clinical Center – Warren Grant Magnuson Clinical Center phone liaison: 301-402-1663

## Gastrointestinal (Gut) Problems

- National Digestive Diseases Information Clearinghouse:
- http://digestive.niddk.nih.gov/

## Hearing and Vision

- National Institute on Deafness and Other Communication Disorders:  www.nidcd.nih.gov/
- American Council for the Blind: http://www.acb.org/index.html
- American Speech-Language-Hearing Association: www.asha.org

## Oral Health

- National Institute for Dental and Craniofacial Research Dental, Oral, and Craniofacial Data Resource Center: http://drc.hhs.gov

## Osteoporosis

- National Institutes of Health for Osteoporosis and Related Bone Diseases, National Resource Center: http://www.niams.nih.gov/Health_Info/Bone/Pain

## Pain

- American Pain Society: www.ampainsoc.org
- American Academy of Pain Medicine: www.painmed.org
- Clinical Trials: www.clinicaltrials.gov

## Stroke and Neurological Diseases

- National Stroke Association: www.stroke.org
- American Stroke Association: www.strokeassociation.org

# Creating Third-Third Transition Learning Environments

## Introduction

From time to time throughout this book, we have suggested that small-group workshops or discussion groups be developed. We have also suggested that these groups be intergenerational whenever possible, in order to provide an environment for women of various ages to learn from one another about a variety of subjects that are of mutual interest. We call these activities "creating TTT learning environments."

These discussion groups might be held at a particular workplace, sponsored by an existing women's organization, convened at a church or synagogue, organized within a specific neighborhood or multiple-family residence, open to the users of a community center, organized around luncheons or dinners, or simply made up of a group of friends and acquaintances who meet in someone's living room or kitchen.

During the women's movement of the 1960s and 1970s, groups like this were called consciousness-raising groups. Today, one women's organization periodically schedules catered "dine-arounds" and small dinners in members' homes. We've heard about boomer groups, retirement planning groups, class reunion groups, women's book groups, and learning circles. Our publisher, Fulcrum Publishing, which is located in Golden, Colorado, is developing and sponsoring a new Third-Third Initiative. In this book, we've suggested that Third-Third Transition (TTT) groups and centers be formed.

In our experience as leaders of innumerable workshops and classes over many years, we would like to suggest a few workshop formats and processes that might be useful to you, our readers, as you consider taking some action along with others at this time of your life.

1. **The Third-Third Transition (TTT) Seminar**. A seminar format is usually designed for a small group in an informal discussion setting.

The group may sit around a conference table or simply arrange chairs in a circle. There is usually a leader, facilitator, or teacher who manages the seminar sessions, but such a person is not required.

The TTT seminar would be designed around one or more specific and relevant Third-Third Transition topics: a discussion of this or another book, retirement planning, financial and investment information, grief and loss, grandparenting, marriage in our older years, health topics, working past age sixty-five, new opportunities for volunteerism, cohousing opportunities, and the like. A common book or article could be read by all the participants. A guest speaker with particular expertise could be invited to make a presentation, followed by questions and answers and discussion. It is likely that one topic will lead to another until a wide array of subjects are addressed.

Academic institutions are often interested in sponsoring seminars, either on a noncredit or academic-credit basis. In this case, there is usually a preset seminar schedule, a means of making announcements about the seminar, and ways of marketing it. If desired, the proceedings and discussions of the seminar can be recorded and later written up as an article, report, or Web-based entry. A video of the seminar could be used in an electronic or television broadcast, distributed as a DVD, or utilized to attract future groups of potential seminar participants.

2. **The Lifecycle Workshop**. The late Daniel J. Levinson, professor of psychology at Yale University and the principal author of *The Seasons of a Man's Life*, developed this format, and coauthor Elinor Greenberg has adapted it in many settings over a number years. The group selects a workshop leader or facilitator. The group participants may sit around one or more tables or just in a circle. However, they must sit in the order of their ages, from youngest to eldest. If the group is large, they might be directed to sit in decade subgroups: twenties, thirties, forties, fifties, and so forth. Be sure that no one is sitting alone. After the group changes their seats according to their ages, they are asked to address common questions: What is the most important issue facing you at this point in your life? How are you approaching this

issue? What would you like say to the people to your right, who just a bit younger than you are? What would you like to say to the people to your left, who are just a bit older than you are?

Give the groups a sufficient amount of time to discuss these questions and come to some consensus, if possible. This could be about a half hour with a fairly large group or just fifteen minutes with a small group. One person is asked to speak for each group, but all the participants may chime in.

When the entire group reconvenes, the workshop leader or facilitator asks each group or each participant, depending on the number of people and the time available, to report their answers to the entire group. The resulting experience is a remarkable recitation of the key issues as they occur throughout the lifecycle. One can envision and recall, like a wave unfolding before one's eyes and ears, the phases of one's own life, as well as be alerted to the issues in the phases of life just ahead. This intergenerational learning process is both satisfying and grounded in reality. It is interesting to note which issues are pretty much expected and which ones come as a surprise, especially to the younger participants.

If time permits, the group can be reconfigured in terms of topics of interest, adjacent age groups, or in any other way that is desirable and feasible. People remark that this workshop is a wonderful and illuminating experience. Often, participants remember the workshop's lessons for many years after the event. This workshop is a true experiential learning activity that helps participants appreciate the entire lifecycle, both in abstract and concrete terms. It is also a nonthreatening way for older participants to share their life lessons and wisdom with younger participants without being pedantic or preachy.

3. **The Third-Third Transition (TTT) Planning Exercise**. Everyone in the intergenerational group agrees to read *A Time of Our Own: In Celebration of Women Over Sixty*. Near the end of Chapter 8, on pages 178 to 181, there is a list of quotes from our interviewees on a number of topics. These quotes are bits of advice offered by the Greatest Generation women to the baby boomers. Everyone is invited to reread the quoted

advice, think about each item, reorganize the items on a piece of paper in any way that suits them, and choose three items that most interest them. That preparation will take about twenty to thirty minutes.

Then the participants choose a partner from an age group other than their own. The intergenerational partners share their three selected items of advice. There will be a total of six items for each pair of partners. The partners discuss their items in pairs and prepare to report back to the larger group.

A key question is posed by the leader or facilitator that each pair of partners must address, for example: Which piece of advice is likely to be the hardest for you to take to heart and follow? Which will be the easiest? Are you ready to discuss with your partner and write a brief TTT plan that focuses on carrying out both the easiest and the hardest pieces of advice? Create a timeline for achieving the goals in your plan, for example, one month, six months, one year, ten years, or longer. It is likely that there will be a variety of ways to organize the topics and items of advice, such as work, leisure, volunteerism, health, finance, and so on.

The partner groups discuss their six items and begin to write down a plan and timeline for addressing at least three of the items they have selected. Each pair of partners reports back to the larger group about their TTT Plans.

It is a bit more complex to ask each partner to report on the other's plan, but there are many advantages in giving that direction: partners become responsible for knowing each other's plans, listening skills are sharpened, and relationships can be built based on shared planning for the future. This tell-about-your-partner's-plan approach is an activity that may lead to friendships, mentorships, and/or mutually supportive e-mails and phone calls, much like the supportive partnerships often forged in "quit smoking" and "quit drinking" groups.

Depending on the nature of the group, it may be possible to reconvene at periodic intervals to check in on the TTT plans. If this exercise is done in a conference setting where participants come from a variety of locations, reconvening may not be feasible. But if this exercise is done in a local organizational setting, then the group could hold periodic TTT planning workshops and support these efforts over a number of years.

It is also possible to use this process without a group, in a one-to-one relationship with a TTT counselor, advisor, coach, or mentor. In that case, individual sessions are planned and the helping party becomes a sounding board for the person in transition. This approach resembles a therapy or counseling session. Colleges and universities as well as social service agencies, religious institutions, and community organizations might offer this type of TTT service to their members and clients.

## Conclusion

These are only a few ideas for utilizing the findings of our study and the sage advice of our interviewees. There are, of course, many more ways to generate and nurture intergenerational life cycle learning. We believe that the time is ripe for these kinds of activities to prosper.

If you have a promising TTT idea that you'd like to share, please send it to us at Ellie.Greenberg@UCHSC.edu or whitney@uwyo.edu.

## Chapter 1: The Third Third of Life

1. R. P. Weathersby and J. M. Tarule, "Life Cycle Stages," *Adult Development: Implications for Higher Education*, AAHE-ERIC Higher Education Research Report No. 4, 1980, American Association for Higher Education.
2. Bernice L. Neugarten, "Personality and Aging," in *Handbook of the Psychology of Aging*, eds. J. E. Birren and K. W. Schaie (New York: Van Nostrand Reinhold, 1977).

## Chapter 2: The Concept of Reinvention

1. US Center for Disease Control, National Center for Health Statistics, *National Vital Statistics Reports* 55, no. 19, August 21, 2007.
2. Jerry Friedman, *Earth's Elders: The Wisdom of the World's Oldest People* (South Kent, CT: Earth's Elders Foundation, Inc., 2005), 73.
3. Ibid., 74.

## Chapter 3: Changing Roles, Responsibilities, and Relationships

1. Term coined by Tom Brokaw in *The Greatest Generation* (New York: Random House, 1998).

## Chapter 4: Women and Work

1. Betty Friedan, *The Feminine Mystique* (New York: W. W. Norton, 1963), 15.
2. Ibid., 32.
3. *Feminists Who Changed America: 1963–1975*, ed. Barbara J. Love (Urbana and Chicago: University of Illinois Press, 2006), xiii.
4. Ibid., xiv–xv.
5. J. M. Tarule, "The Process of Transformation," in *Educating Learners of All Ages, New Directions for Higher Education*, no. 29, Elinor Miller Greenberg, Kathleen O'Donnell, and William Bergquist (San Francisco: Jossey-Bass, 1980), 23–25.

6. US WEST Strategic Planning documents, 1997.

7. JVA Consulting, *Boomers Leading Change: Ages 55–64* (Denver, CO: Rose Community Foundation, 2007).

8. "Extra! Baby Boomer Capital," *Rocky Mountain News* (Denver, CO), April 7, 2007, hometodenver.com/stats-Denver.htm, 4.

9. For example, Frances Wisebart Jacobs (1843–1892), called "The Mother of Charities," established, along with four clergymen, the Charity Organization Society, the interfaith predecessor to the Community Chest, in 1887, in Denver, Colorado. This effort later became the multiagency organization known as the Mile Hi United Way.

10. Marc Freedman, *Prime Time: How Baby Boomers Will Revolutionize Retirement and Transform America* (New York: PublicAffairs, 1999).

## Chapter 5: Women and Money

1. US National Center for Disease Control, National Center for Health Statistics, *National Vital Statistics Reports* 55, no. 19 (August 21, 2007).

2. Karlyn Bowman and Ruy Teixeira, "The Search for the Next Soccer Mom," *Wall Street Journal*, February 28, 2008, A17. Data from Tom Smith, National Opinion Research Center.

3. 2007 Mom Salary Survey, www.salary.com, reported by Ellen Goodman from *The Boston Globe* in the *Rocky Mountain News* (Denver, CO), May 12, 2007, and Mike Rosen in *The Denver Post*, May 11, 2007.

4. US Census, reported in the *Rocky Mountain News* (Denver, CO), April 25, 2007.

5. US Department of Labor, reported in the *Rocky Mountain News* (Denver, CO), April 25, 2007.

6. American Association of University Women, "Behind the Pay Gap," reported in the *Rocky Mountain News* (Denver, CO), April 23, 2007. To view the report, see www.aauw.org.

7. Colorado General Assembly, reported in *The Denver Post*, April 24, 2007.

8. Frank Greve, "Marriages Working Because Wives Are," *The Denver Post*, May 23, 2007, 4C.

9. P. R. Amato, A. Booth, D. R. Johnson, and S. J. Rodgers, *Alone Together: How Marriage in America Is Changing* (Boston: Harvard University Press, 2007).

10. David Crary, "Divorce in U.S. at 37-Year Low," *Rocky Mountain News* (Denver, CO), May 11, 2007, and David Crary, "'I Do' Sticking—Divorce Rate Falls," *The Denver Post,* May 11, 2007.

11. Andrew Cherlin, in "Divorce in U.S. at 37-Year Low" by David Crary, *Rocky Mountain News* (Denver, CO), May 11, 2007.


**Chapter 6: Women and Health**

1. John Rowe and Robert L. Kahn, *Successful Aging: The MacArthur Study* (New York: Dell Publishing/Random House, 1998).

2. L. Fried and J. Walston, "Fraility and Failure to Thrive," in *Principles of Geriatic Medicine and Gerontology,* eds. W. Hazzard, J. Blass, W. Ettinger, J. Halter, and J. Ouslander (New York: McGraw-Hill, 1999), 1308–1402.

3. American Geriatrics Society Panel on Persistent Pain in Older Persons, "The Management of Persistent Pain in Older Persons," *Journal of the American Geriatrics Society* 50, no. 1 (2002): 205–224.

4. Helena Chiu, "Cardiovascular Disease," in *The Encyclopedia of Aging,* 3rd ed., ed. George L. Maddox (New York: Springer Publishing Company, 2001), 191–194, and Shawana Freshwater and Charles Golden, "Stroke," in *The Encyclopedia of Aging,* 3rd ed., ed. George L. Maddox (New York: Springer Publishing Company, 2001), 982–984.

5. K. Shay and J. A. Ship, "The Importance of Oral Health in the Older Patient," *Journal of the American Geriatics Society* 43 (1995): 1414–1422.

6. Centers for Disease Control and Prevention, *National Diabetes Fact Sheet: General Information and National Estimates on Diabetes in the United States* (Atlanta: US Department of Health and Human Services, Centers for Disease Control and Prevention, 2005).

7. G. S. Meneilly, *The Oxford Textbook of Geriatric Medicine,* 2nd ed., eds. J. Grimley Evans, T. F. Williams, L. F. Beattie, J. P. Michel, and G. K. Wilcock (New York: Oxford University Press, 2000), 210–217.

8. National Institutes of Health, "Osteoporosis Prevention, Diagnosis and Therapy," *Journal of the American Medical Association* 285, no. 6 (2001): 785–795.

9. Lodovice Balducci, "Cancer in the Older Person," *Generations* 30, no. 3 (Fall 2006): 45–50.

10. Ibid., 48.

11. Robert D. Hill, *Positive Aging: A Guide for Mental Health Professionals and Counselors* (New York: W. W. Norton, 2005); John W. Rowe and Robert L. Kahn, *Successful Aging* (New York: Pantheon Books), 1998; and *The Encyclopedia of Aging*, 3rd ed., ed. George L. Maddox (New York: Springer Publishing Company, 2001).

12. Hill, *Positive Aging*, 52–54.

13. E. H. Erikson, J. M. Erikson, and H. O. Kivnick, *Vital Involvement in Old Age* (New York: W. W. Norton, 1986), and Hill, *Positive Aging*, 25.

14. Hill, *Positive Aging*, 52.

15. Hill, *Positive Aging*, 96–118. Author's note: The information in these two pages was adapted by Fay Wadsworth Whitney from the reference cited here. The full text has been shortened considerably but maintains the integrity of catagorization and major ideas of the original author.

### Chapter 7: Losses, Regrets, and Gains

1. Elinor Miller Greenberg, "Becoming a Parent to your Parent," Notes from the Everyday, *Arapahoe Independent* (Littleton, CO), November 27, 1979, reprinted in Elinor Miller Greenberg, *Weaving: The Fabric of a Woman's Life* (Littleton, CO: EMG and Associates, 1991), 87–89.

2. M. E. P. Seligman and M. Csikszentmhatyi, "Positive Psychology: An Introduction," *American Psychologist* 55 (2000): 5–14.

3. Elinor Miller Greenberg, "For Bert Langfur" in *Weaving: The Fabric of a Woman's Life* (Littleton, CO: EMG and Associates, 1991), 123–126.

4. Greenberg, "Inner Voices: Mickey and Ellie" (unpublished paper, May 29, 1991).

5. Greenberg, "The Last Tomorrow" (unpublished paper, May 29, 1991).

6. Greenberg, "Our Friend Has Died" (unpublished paper, May 29, 1991).

7. Erik H. Erikson, "Identity and the Life Cycle," *Psychological Issues* Monograph 1, (New York: International Universities Press, 1959).

### Chapter 8: From Generation to Generation

1. Karen Rouse, "Moving on with Life," *The Denver Post,* July 25, 2007, 1C. (Rouse's data source is the North Carolina Division of Aging and Adult Services.)

2. Tom Brokaw, *The Greatest Generation* (New York: Random House, 1998).

3. Jane Glenn Haas, "Women's Voices on Retirement: Older and Wiser," in *Generations: Journal of the American Society on Aging* (Summer 2002): 83.

4. Ibid.; www.womansage.com.

5. "Boomers Leading Change," a community assessment conducted by the Rose Community Foundation with support from The Atlantic Philanthropies, Denver, Colorado, 2007. www.coloradoboomers.com.

6. Ibid.

7. Tom McGhee, "Most Boomers Not Ready to Retire," *The Denver Post,* June 28, 2007, 3C.

8. Harold Ford Jr., Merrill Lynch vice chairman and senior policy advisor, former US congressman, in *Merrill Lynch Advisor,* June 2007, 15.

9. George Santayana, *Life of Reason* (New York: Scribner's, 1905), 284.

**Chapter 9: From a Room of Our Own to a Time of Our Own**

1. Richard Stengel, "A Time to Serve," *Time*, September 10, 2007, 48–67.

2. Ibid.

3. Marc Freedman, *Encore: Finding Work That Matters in the Second Half of Life* (New York: PublicAffairs, 2007), 166–200.

# Re/ource/

Albom, Mitch. *Tuesdays with Morrie: An Old Man and Life's Greatest Lesson.* New York: Random House, 1997.

Amato, P. R., A. Booth, D. R. Johnson, and S. J. Rodgers. *Alone Together: How Marriage in America Is Changing.* Boston: Harvard University Press, 2007.

American Association of University Women. "Behind the Pay Gap." Research report, reported in the *Rocky Mountain News* (Denver, CO), April 23, 2007. (Also available at www.aauw.org.)

American Geriatrics Society Panel on Persistent Pain in Older Persons. "The Management of Persistent Pain in Older Persons." *Journal of the American Geriatrics Society* 50 (1): 205–224.

Balducci, Lodovice "Cancer in the Older Person." *Generations* 30 (3): 45–50.

Bateson, Mary Catherine. *Composing a Life.* New York: The Atlantic Monthly Press, 1989.

Belenky, Mary Field, Blythe McVicker Clinchy, Nancy Rule Goldberger, and Jill Mattuck Tarule. *Women's Ways of Knowing: The Development of Self, Voice, and Mind.* New York: Basic Books, 1986.

Bergquist, William H., Elinor Miller Greenberg, and G. Alan Klaum. *In Our Fifties: Voices of Men and Women Reinventing Their Lives.* San Francisco: Jossey-Bass, 1993.

Boulieu, Etienne-Emile, interview by Charlie Rose. *Charlie Rose*, PBS, January 4, 2007.

Bridges, William. *The Way of Transition: Embracing Life's Most Difficult Moments.* Cambridge, MA: Perseus, 2001.

Brokaw, Tom. *The Greatest Generation.* New York: Random House, 1998.

———. *The Greatest Generation Speaks: Letters and Reflections.* New York: Random House, 1999.

Buch, Linda J. "Senior Class: Programs Prove You're Never Too Old to Get Fit and Have Fun." *The Denver Post,* July 30, 2007, 1E.

Bunch, Joey. "A Silver Tsunami: Metro Area's Flood of Aging Residents to Pit

Seniors vs. Kids for Public Funds." *The Denver Post*, June 11, 2007, 1A.

Centers for Disease Control and Prevention. *National Diabetes Fact Sheet: General Information and National Estimates on Diabetes in the United States.* Atlanta: US Department of Health and Human Services, Centers for Disease Control and Prevention, 2005. www.cdc.gov/diabetes/pubs/pdf/ndfs_2005.pdf.

Chickering, Arthur W. "Development as a Major Outcome." In *Experiential Learning: Rationale, Characteristics and Assessment.* Ed. Morris T. Keeton. San Francisco: Jossey-Bass, 1976.

———, ed. *The Modern American College: Responding to the New Realities of Diverse Students and a Changing Society.* San Francisco: Jossey-Bass, 1981.

Chickering, Arthur W., and Robert J. Havighurst. "The Life Cycle." In *The Modern American College: Responding to the Realities of Diverse Students and a Changing Society.* Ed. Arthur W. Chickering. San Francisco: Jossey-Bass 1981.

Chiu, Helena. "Cardiovascular Disease." In *The Encyclopedia of Aging.* 3rd ed. Ed. George L. Maddox. New York: Springer Publishing Company, 2001.

Crary, David. "Divorce in U.S. at 37-Year Low." *Rocky Mountain News* (Denver, CO), May 11, 2007.

———. "'I Do' Sticking—Divorce Rate Falls." *The Denver Post*, May 11, 2007.

Downs, Marion P. *Shut Up and Live! (You Know How): A 93-Year-Old's Guide to Living to a Ripe Old Age.* New York: Avery, 2007.

Elders, Joyceln. "Health and Health Care." In *Earth's Elders: The Wisdom of the World's Oldest People.* South Kent, CT: Earth's Elders Foundation, 2005.

Equal Pay Day-House Joint Resolution 1046, Colorado General Assembly, "Go Figure," *The Denver Post*, April 24, 2007.

Erikson, Erik H. *Childhood and Society.* 2nd ed. New York: W. W. Norton, 1950, 1963.

———. "Identity and the Life Cycle." *Psychological Issues* Monograph 1. New York: International Universities Press, 1959.

———. "The Life Cycle: Epigenesis of Identity." In *Identity: Youth and Crisis.*

New York: W. W. Norton, 1968.

Erikson, E. H., J. M. Erikson, and H. O. Kivnick. *Vital Involvement in Old Age*. New York: W. W. Norton, 1986.

Foster, Mark S. *Citizen Quigg: A Mayor's Life of Civic Service*. Golden, CO: Fulcrum Publishing, 2006.

Ford, Harold, Jr., *Merrill Lynch Advisor*, June 2007, 15.

Freedman, Marc. *Encore: Finding Work That Matters in the Second Half of Life*. New York: PublicAffairs, 2007.

———. *Prime Time: How Baby Boomers Will Revolutionize Retirement and Transform America*. New York: PublicAffairs, 1999.

Freshwater, Shawana, and Charles Golden. "Stroke." In *The Encyclopedia of Aging*. 3rd ed. Ed. George L. Maddox. New York:  Springer Publishing Company, 2001.

Fried, L., and J. Walston. "Frailty and Failure to Thrive." In *Principles of Geriatic Medicine and Gerontology*. Eds. W. Hazzard, J. Blass, W. Ettinger, J. Halter, and J. Ouslander. New York: McGraw-Hill, 1999.

Friedan, Betty. *The Feminine Mystique*. New York: W. W. Norton, 1963.

———. *Life So Far: A Memoir*. New York: Simon & Schuster, 2000.

Friedman, Jerry. *Earth's Elders: The Wisdom of the World's Oldest People*. South Kent, CT: Earth's Elders Foundation, 2005.

Gould, Roger L. "Adult Life Stages: Growth toward Self-Tolerance." *Psychology Today* 8 (February 1975): 74–78.

———. *Transformations: Growth and Change in Adult Life*. New York: Simon & Schuster, 1978.

Greenberg, Elinor Miller. "Becoming a Parent to Your Parent," *Arapahoe Independent* (Littleton, CO), November 27, 1979.

———. "Hurry Up! You're Late!" *Arapahoe Independent* (Littleton, CO), October 28, 1980.

———. "In Our 60's." *Women's Business News* (Denver, CO), 1 (2) (October 1995).

———. "Quality Lifelong Education: New Perspectives on Design and Administration." PhD diss. Ann Arbor, MI: University Microfilms International, 1981.

———. "Time." *Arapahoe Independent* (Littleton, CO), January 20, 1981.

———. *Weaving: The Fabric of a Woman's Life*, Littleton, CO: EMG and Associates, 1991.

Greenberg, Elinor Miller, Kathleen M. O'Donnell, and William Bergquist, eds. *Educating Learners of All Ages, New Directions for Higher Education*. San Francisco: Jossey-Bass, 1980.

Greenberg, Elinor Miller, with Lois J. Zachary. "Stopping Out Is In!" *Adult Learning* 2 (4): 24–26.

Greve, Frank. "Marriages Working Because Wives Are." *The Denver Post*, May 23, 2007, 4C.

Haas, Jane Glenn, "Women's Voices on Retirement: Older and Wiser." *Generations: Journal of the American Society on Aging* 26 (11): 83–85.

Havighurst, Robert J. *Developmental Tasks and Education*. 3rd ed. New York: McKay, 1972.

Hill, Robert D. *Positive Aging: A Guide for Mental Health Professionals and Consumers*. New York: W. W. Norton, 2005.

Johnson, Mary, ed. "Retirement: New Chapters in American Life." *Generations: Journal of the American Society on Aging* 26 (11).

JVA Consulting. "Boomers Leading Change: Ages 55–64." Denver: Rose Community Foundation, April 10, 2007.

Lamm, Dottie. *Daddy on Board: Parenting Roles for the 21st Century*. Golden, CO: Fulcrum Publishing, 2007.

Levinson, Daniel J. *The Seasons of a Man's Life*. New York: Alfred A. Knopf, 1978.

Love, Barbara J., ed. *Feminists Who Changed America: 1963–1975*. Urbana and Chicago: University of Illinois Press, 2006.

Maddox, George L., ed. *The Encyclopedia of Aging*. 3rd ed. New York: Springer Publishing Company, 2001.

Martz, Sandra Halderman, ed. *If I Had My Life to Live Over, I Would Pick More Daisies*. Watsonville, CA: Papier-Mache Press, 1992.

McGhee, Tom. "Most Boomers Not Ready to Retire." *The Denver Post*, June 28, 2007, 3C.

Mellor, M. Joanna, and Helen Rehr. *Baby Boomers: Can My Eighties Be Like My Fifties?* New York: Springer Publishing Company, 2005.

Meneilly, G. S. In *The Oxford Textbook of Geriatric Medicine*. 2nd. ed. Eds.

J. Grimley Evans, T. F. Williams, L. F. Beattie, J. P. Michel, and G. K. Wilcock. New York: Oxford University Press, 2000.

National Institutes of Health. "Osteoporosis Prevention, Diagnosis and Therapy," *Journal of the American Medical Association* 285 (6): 785–795.

Neugarten, Bernice L. "Personality and Aging." In *Handbook of the Psychology of Aging.* Eds. E. Birren and K. W. Schaie. New York: Van Nostrand Reinhold, 1977.

Neugarten, Bernice L. *Middle Age and Aging: Reader in Social Psychology.* Chicago: University of Chicago Press, 1968.

Quintera, Fernando. "Boomers Don't Plan to Slow Down." *Rocky Mountain News* (Denver, CO), June 28, 2007, 40.

Rosenthal, Jack. "On Language: Words for the New Age of Age." *New York Times,* July 22, 2007, magazine section, 16.

Rountree, Cathleen. *On Women Turning 60: Embracing the Age of Fulfillment.* New York: Three Rivers Press, 1997.

Rouse, Karen. "Moving on with Life." *The Denver Post,* July 25, 2007, 1C.

Rowe, John W., and Robert L. Kahn. *Successful Aging.* New York: Pantheon Books, 1998.

Seligman, M. E. P., and M. Csikszentmhatyi. "Positive Psychology: An Introduction." *American Psychologist* 55: 5–14.

Shay, K., and J. A. Ship. "The Importance of Oral Health in the Older Patient." *Journal of the American Geriatics Society* 43: 1414–1422.

Sheehy, Gail. *New Passages: Mapping Life across Time.* New York: Random House, 1995.

———. *Passages: Predictable Crises of Adult Life.* New York: E. P. Dutton & Co., 1974.

Stengel, Richard. "A Time to Serve." *Time,* September 10, 2007.

Tarule, J. M. "The Process of Transformation." In *Educating Learners of All Ages, New Directions for Higher Education.* No. 29. Eds. Elinor Miller Greenberg, Kathleen O'Donnell, and William Bergquist. San Francisco: Jossey-Bass, 1980.

Tobias, Sheila. *Faces of Feminism: An Activist's Reflections on the Women's Movement.* Boulder, CO: Westview Press, 1997.

Tocqueville, Alexis de. *Democracy in America.* Ed. J. P. Mayer, trans. George

Lawrence. New York: Harper and Row, 1969.

Trafford, Abigail. *My Time: Making the Most of the Bonus Decades after Fifty.* New York: Basic Books, 2004.

Weathersby, Rita P., and J. M. Tarule. *Adult Development: Implications for Higher Education.* AAHE-ERIC Higher Education Research Report No. 4. Washington, DC: American Association for Higher Education, 1980.

## Websites

http://adultdevelopment.org

www.coloradoboomers.com

www.elderhostel.org

www.dareassociation.org

www.grantcountyseniorservices.org

www.myseniors.com

www.positiveaging.com

www.silverplanet.com

www.3rdThird.org

www.womansage.com

## Archives

Elinor Miller Greenberg Collection. Littleton Historical Museum, Littleton, CO. www.littletongov.org/museum.

Elinor Miller Greenberg Papers. Dayton Memorial Library, Regis University, Denver, CO. www.regis.edu.

**Elinor "Ellie" Miller Greenberg** is president and CEO of EMG and Associates, a Colorado-based national consulting and publishing firm. She began her more than fifty-year career as a speech pathologist. During the civil rights movement, she cofounded the Littleton Council for Human Relations and brought Dr. Martin Luther King Jr. to her community. During the women's movement, she was the founding director and national coordinator of the University Without Walls at Loretto Heights College. She was the founding administrator of PATHWAYS to the Future at US WEST and the Mountain and Plains Partnership at the University of Colorado Health Sciences Center. Currently, she consults with education and judicial projects and serves on community organization boards. She has served on state commissions under two Colorado governors.

Greenberg authored *Weaving: The Fabric of a Woman's Life* (1991) and *A Journey for Justice* (1993), coauthored *Designing Undergraduate Education* (1981) and *In Our Fifties: Voices of Men and Women Reinventing Their Lives* (1993), and is a featured columnist for www.silverplanet.com.

She holds a BA from Mount Holyoke College, an MA from the University of Wisconsin, and an EdD from the University of Northern Colorado and has received two honorary doctorates and many other honors.

Greenberg has been married for fifty-three years and has three grown children and four grandchildren.

**Fay Wadsworth Whitney** is professor emeritus in nursing at the Fay W. Whitney School of Nursing at the University of Wyoming in Laramie. She began her forty-seven-year nursing career as a psychiatric nurse at Strong Memorial Hospital in Rochester, New York. After a thirteen-year "stop out" to raise three children and run The Funny Farm Stable in Pompei, New York, for young riders and their horses, her nursing career turned to community-based health and education. Working with state legislators and appointed to state and national committees and commissions, she helped to pass enabling national legislation for new advanced nursing care by nurse practitioners. Currently, she advocates for health care reforms through membership on state commissions in New York, Pennsylvania, Wyoming, and nationally.

Since the 1970s, Fay has focused on developing innovative education programs for nurses. Being among the first adult nurse practitioners in the nation, her goal has been to develop improved interdisciplinary primary care through education, service, and research.

She holds a BSN from the University of Rochester and a MSN, MPh, and PhD from Syracuse University. She has received several honors in teaching, research, and practice over her long collaborative health career.

Whitney has been married for forty-nine years and has three married children and ten grandchildren.

"Yes, we should celebrate! We are the first generation of women to reach their sixties in good health and ready to exhale and do what we want! A great read! You'll love it!"

—Patricia S. Schroeder, president and CEO of the Association of American Publishers and former congresswoman

"Greenberg and Whitney are masters of the picture-window interview: open ended, empathetic, focused without being didactic. Their goal is to tell the reader not what to think, but what to think about."

—Sheila Tobias, author of *Faces of Feminism: An Activist's Reflections on the Women's Movement*

"Greenberg and Whitney provide a wealth of information for those of us in our 'third third,' which, given lengthening life spans, is likely to be the longest of the three. We've had it all—wife and mother, home manager, successful volunteer, and career woman—with the accompanying intellectual challenges, income, satisfaction, and fun. Now we must reinvent ourselves once more. *A Time of Our Own* offers valuable insights in how to do so."

—Tucker Hart Adams, president, The Adams Group Inc.

"It is hard to believe that this book is not a 500-page tome: it contains everything we might want in our older years and deals sensitively with every event of our life's journey. I strongly recommend it to women over sixty, sons, daughters, and partners, and professionals in all health-related disciplines."

—Claire M. Fagin, PhD, RN, dean emerita; professor emerita; interim president emerita, Claire M. Fagin Hall, University of Pennsylvania